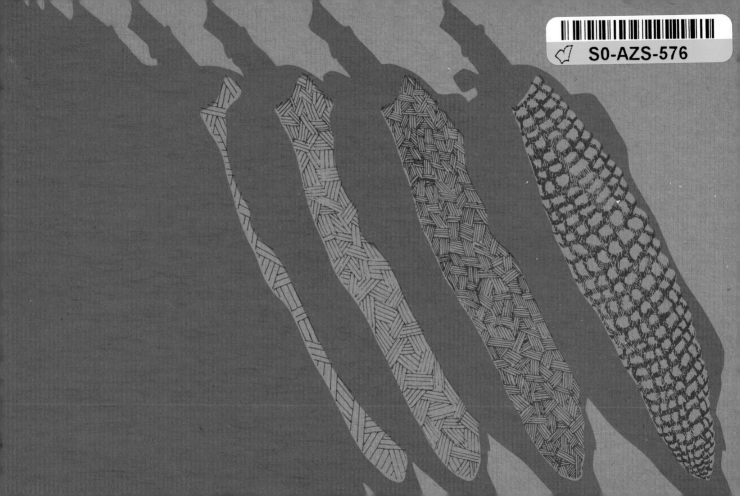
S0-AZS-576

books designed with giving in mind

Kid's Pets Book
Make It Ahead
   French Cooking
Soups & Stews
Crepes & Omelets
Microwave Cooking
Vegetable Cookbook
Kid's Arts and Crafts
Bread Baking
The Crockery Pot Cookbook
Kid's Garden Book
Classic Greek Cooking

The Compleat American
   Housewife 1776
Low Carbohydrate Cookbook
Kid's Cookbook
Italian
Cheese Guide & Cookbook
Miller's German
Quiche & Souffle
To My Daughter, With Love
Natural Foods
Chinese Vegetarian
Jewish Gourmet
Working Couples

Mexican
Sunday Breakfast
Fisherman's Wharf Cookbook
Charcoal Cookbook
Ice Cream Cookbook
Hippo Hamburger
Blender Cookbook
The Wok, a Chinese Cookbook
Cast Iron Cookbook
Japanese Country
Fondue Cookbook
Food Processor Cookbook
Peanuts & Popcorn

from nitty gritty productions

DEDICATED TO . . .

Diane Rose, who introduced me to natural foods.

Fred Rohe, who, by hiring me to tell others about natural foods, gave me the chance to learn all about them myself.

David Sawle, whose enthusiasm for my stuffed cabbage leaves and carob mousse encouraged me to write this book.

Jane Kronholtz, who has urged me on for half my lifetime.

My parents, who gave me the freedom to do — or try to do — anything.

Maxine Atwater
San Francisco, 1972

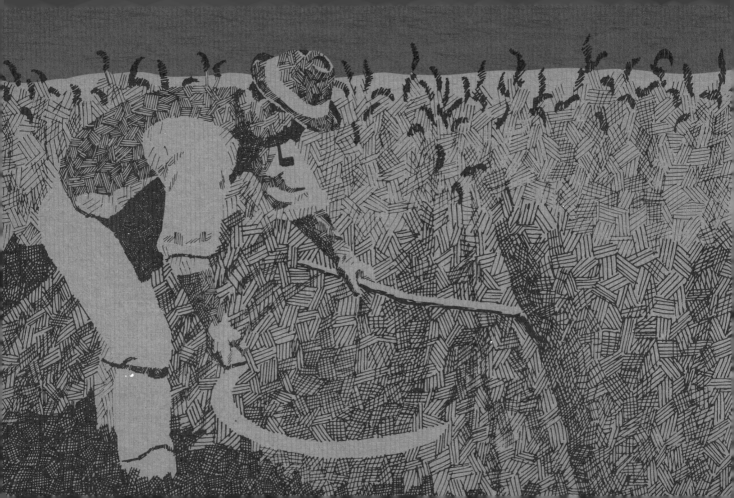

Natural Foods cookbook

by Maxine Atwater

Illustrations by Craig Torlucci

© Copyright 1972
Nitty Gritty Productions
Concord, California

A Nitty Gritty Book*
Published by
Nitty Gritty Productions
P.O. Box 5457
Concord, California 94524

*Nitty Gritty Books - Trademark
Owned by Nitty Gritty Productions
Concord, California

ISBN 0-911954-21-X

Table of Contents

Introduction

The revolution toward a better way of life has begun. Organically-grown foods, foods that are unprocessed and as close to their natural state as possible, lead the way. Already beans are sprouting, home-made yogurt is incubating and wholewheat flour is grinding in hearth-side hand mills while juicers chomp on home-grown vegetables throughout America.

A myriad of natural food markets offer all the ingredients: crocks, pots, barrels, bins, shelves, and dairy cases loaded with everything from azuki beans and fenugreek seeds, to honey, yogurt, wheat germ, tamari, and sesame oil.

Everything's there, ready to enrich bodies, create new energy and vitality, probably to change the way people feel and how they think about the world.

The question for many is 'how'?

"How do I use these natural foods?" cooks ask, recipe boxes lovingly in hand. "How can I join the natural food revolution and take my favorite recipes along?"

The answer is easy — substitute. Use a bit of this in place of that; add a little of a particularly nutritious natural food and leave out something that's nutritionally questionable.

You can learn these 'hows' by studying this book, then taking the principles and experimenting on your own to create familiar flavors and textures. Hopefully, many of your favorite recipes will be here, already converted for you to make the way easier.

Happy, healthy eating, dear friend, and welcome to the revolution!

M.H.A. 1972

Substitution Table

In place of:	Use instead:
bouillon	tamari, kombu, water (see page 3)
bread crumbs	softened soy grits or wheat germ
chocolate	carob
processed cheese	natural cheese
coffee	Yano
cornstarch	arrowroot
commercial eggs	fertile eggs
flour, white	
unbleached	
'enriched'	wholewheat flour or wholewheat pastry flour
gelatin	agar-agar flakes/sticks
margarine	butter or corn germ oil
mayonnaise	Tofu mayonnaise (see page 6 & 7) or part mayonnaise and part yogurt

milk	milk plus additional milk powder
noodles	wholewheat noodles
oil	unrefined oils, preferably cold-pressed
pepper	paprika
salt	sea salt, sesame salt, vege-salt, tamari
shortening	butter or unrefined oil
sour cream	yogurt
soy sauce	tamari plus water
sugar	honey, date sugar, apple concentrate
tomato juice	fresh tomatoes, lemon juice (see page 9)
vinegar	lemon juice or apple cider vinegar
white rice	whole-grain brown rice, grown organically

Stock Your Shelves

agar-agar flakes — use in place of gelatin 2 t. to each 2-3 cups liquid.

arrowroot — natural thickening agent, in place of cornstarch.

apple concentrate — use as non-sugar sweetener, especially in fruit dishes.

carob — if recipe calls for square of chocolate, use 3 T carob + 2 T water.

cheese, natural — without preservatives, keep covered in refrigerator.

corn germ oil — vitamin rich, tastes like butter for baking.

eggs, fertile — rich in enzymes, estrogenic hormones and lecithin.

honey, unrefined — fine natural sweetener without detrimental effects of sugar. Use variety — clover, avocado, tulepo, orange.

kelp — vitamins and minerals naturally balanced. Use especially with fish.

milk, powdered/non-instant — 1 part powder to 4 parts water in place of standard milk. Concentrated protein.

miso — protein made from soy beans, use in soups at end of cooking.

nuts, raw — concentrated vegetable protein. Make nut butter and nut milk.

nutritional or brewers yeast — great protein source. Use 1 or 2 T. in any stuffing, loaf or sauce. Torumel brand is mildest.

oils, unrefined — unsaturated vegetable oils, sesame, sunflower, peanut, walnut, safflower; extracted without heat.

rice, whole grain, brown — always use instead of white rice.

sea salt — obtained from sea water, rich in minerals including calcium.

seeds, sunflower/sesame — add seeds to baked goods, entrees and desserts.

sesame salt — made from sea salt and sesame meal.

soy grits — the cracked soy bean offers more than twice the protein of meat.

tamari — soy sauce fermented for 2 years in kegs; use in soup, vegetables or rice.

tofu — soy bean curd, rich protein supplement. Keep in water in refrigerator.

vege-salt — mineral-rich. Made from sea salt and vegetables.

yano — coffee substitute made from grain.

wheat germ — rich in protein, vitamins E, B, and iron.

wholewheat flour — buy freshly milled wheat just before using.

wholewheat noodles — and sesame flour noodles. Refrigerate.

yogurt — unsweetened, additive-free, or make your own.

Basic Ingredients

Before you begin cooking up a heavenly storm with natural foods, try to have on hand some of the basics. Prepare your own Granola, a healthy combination of oats, seeds, coconut, nuts as a topping for almost any dessert and as the ideal snack. Grind those nuts to make nut butter and nut milk. Lay in a supply of long-grain brown rice that's been grown organically. Begin sprouting your alfalfa seeds, mung beans, and wheat. Make up a batch of your own mayonnaise once a week. And don't forget the vegetable and meat-base bouillon stocks for soups and sauces. With these basics in your refrigerator and cupboards, you'll be ready to cook the natural way.

GRANOLA DESSERT TOPPING/SNACK

2-1/2 c rolled oats
1/4 c sesame seed
1/4 c sunflower seed
1/2 c coconut
1/2 c wheat germ, untoasted

1/2 c nuts, chopped
1/3 c water
1/2 c honey
1/3 c oil

Mix all ingredients and spread about 2 inches thick on a shallow pan. Bake at 225° for 2 hours. Store in lidded jars or plastic bags.

NUT BUTTER

Nut butter can be substituted for some or all of the butter called for in many recipes. Using a blender, pulverize 1-2 cups raw nuts. Add a vegetable salt and enough oil to make a paste. Refrigerate.

LONG-GRAIN BROWN RICE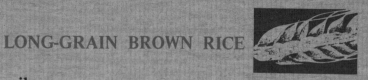

1 c long-grain brown rice   2 T oil
2 c water   1 t sea salt

Wash the rice under water. Bring the water to a boil and add the oil and the salt. Slowly add the rice so boiling does not stop. Cook gently for 45 minutes or until grains have absorbed all liquid. Serves 6.

BOUILLON

To avoid the additives in commercial bouillon, make your own. Classic bouillon, like Grandma used to make, involves simmering beef bones in water and then adding herbs, onions, garlic, and perhaps a touch of Tabasco. You can do the same, even experimenting by adding leftover meat scraps and bones.

SPROUTS

Together with wholewheat flour, honey and yogurt, sprouts head the list as the natural food advocates' most important daily fare.

This living food, miraculously given forth by the seemingly dormant seed, bean, or kernel of grain, long has brought nourishment to other cultures. Now in the United States people are beginning to tap this storehouse — the plants' cherished supply of minerals, vitamins, and proteins set aside for future generations.

Most seeds, beans, and grains, when sprouted, double or triple in vitamin, mineral, and protein content. And these nutrition rich sprouts taste good, adding new texture, color, and freshness to salads, soups, and entrees. Although almost any seed, bean, or grain can be sprouted, most popular are alfalfa, sunflower and fenugreek seeds, lentil beans, wheat and rye grains.

To join the sprouting fun, put seeds, beans, or grain into a glass jar, cover with water, and stretch a piece of cheese cloth around the mouth, fastening it with rubber bands, and let stand overnight. In the morning pour off the water, then tilt the jar so excess water will trickle off. Place the jar in a dark, ventilated cupboard. Rinse the sprouts two or three times a day, tilting the jar again each time.

Refer to the chart for amounts of seeds, beans, or grain to use with each quart of water and for the number of days sprouting takes for each variety:

Seed/Bean/Grain	Proportion	Time	Length
lentils	3/4 cup	3 days	½-1"
sunflower	1 cup	2 days	¼"
mung beans	3/4 cup	2-3 days	2-3"
alfalfa	3 T	3-4 days	1-2"
wheat	1 cup	2 days	¼-½"
fenugreek	1 cup	3 days	½-1"
rye	1 cup	3-4 days	¼-½"

When sprouts are proper length use them from the jar — beans, sprouts and all.

 **MAYONNAISE**

2 T butter
1/2 c wholewheat pastry flour
1 c water
2 egg yolks
1/2 c honey
1 t vege-salt
1/2 t dry mustard
2 t vinegar
2 T lemon juice
1/4 t cayenne
1 c safflower or peanut oil

Melt butter in sauce pan, blend in flour then slowly add water. Bring to a boil and cook, stirring constantly until thick.

Blend or mix remaining ingredients. Gradually add the hot mixture. Let cool and refrigerate.

TOFU MAYONNAISE

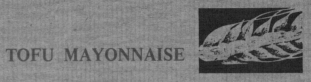

1 square (2 lbs) Tofu
1/2 c olive oil
1/2 c vinegar
1/2 t dill
1/2 t honey
1 t sea salt

Liquefy Tofu in blender. Add oil slowly, then seasonings, vinegar, and honey. Taste, and add more honey if too tart; add more vinegar if not tart enough. This mayonnaise cannot be heated or it will separate, but it can be used as a topping for hot vegetables if added after vegetables are off the heat. Tofu mayonnaise to which 1 teaspoon caraway has been added makes a delightful binder for cold slaw. Use Tofu mayonnaise seasoned with tarragon on cold vegetables.

VEGETABLE STOCK

Many recipes call for stock or a vegetable-base liquid. Instead of using a vegetable bouillon cube which contains additives, make your own.

Leftover vegetable parings, outer leaves — any part of the vegetable you usually discard — can be used to make stock. Save these leftovers in a plastic bag in the refrigerator until you have a quantity, then add them to boiling water, cover and simmer for 15 minutes. Strain off the liquid and keep in a jar in the refrigerator to use as a basis for soup and for those many recipes calling for stock or water. Add to this jar all vegetable cooking water. You'll be getting a rich portion of water soluble vitamins at no cost.

TOMATO JUICE/SAUCE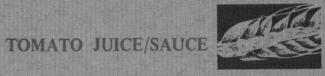

Since many classic recipes call for tomato juice or tomato sauce, it's good to know that you can make your own rather than rely on the canned varieties that contain additives. To make tomato juice, simply puree tomatoes in a blender, add lemon juice and salt. Strain the mixture for juice and retain the pulp and a little juice to use in recipes calling for tomato sauce.

NUT MILK

A milk made from raw nuts and water can often be used in place of dairy milk. To make a nut milk, liquefy one cup of raw peanuts, cashews, or blanched almonds with 4 cups of water in a blender. Add 2 T honey, molasses, or pitted dates for sweetness; decrease water for a creamier milk.

Appetizers

Munching and nibbling — a snack here, a tidbit there. Welcome to 20th Century America. As a way of life, the between-meal snack is in. For times when an exciting TV show, or friends dropping in, seems to demand something to eat, be sure you have on hand the best of all possible snacks.

When no one's looking and when you're feeling particularly strong-willed, toss out those nothing foods in your cupboard and refrigerator. In place of the additive-heavy crackers and chips, the prepackaged cereals, the boxes of sugar-coated snacks, fill your shelves with bags of popcorn kernels, whole grain crackers, dried fruits, including raisins and dates, nuts in the shell, honey-coated treats, and a tin of carob powder for making a chocolate-like milk drink. Have a cereal snack in the refrigerator, such as the granola on page 2.

For between-meal snacks and before dinner appetizers, set out trays of iced fresh cucumber strips, green onions, pepper circles, tomato wedges, cauliflower florets, radishes, carrot sticks, and mushrooms. With the raw vegetables, serve bowls of creamy yogurt mixed with Blue cheese and garlic for dipping. On festive occasions bring on a board of soft cheeses, nut butters, and wholewheat crackers.

When it's party time or you want to serve before-dinner nibbles with zesty vegetable juice or dry sherry aperitifs, choose from the recipes that follow or adapt your own favorite hors d'oeuvres and canapes to natural foods.

Generally, substitute wholewheat flour and bread for white flour and white bread. Use unrefined oils and butter in place of margarine and other hydrogenated oils. Use yogurt in place of sour cream, and make your own mayonnaise. Instead of regular salt use sea salt, tamari, vege-salt, or sesame salt. Add a half cup of powdered milk to almost any recipe calling for milk. Substitute wheat germ for bread crumbs. Use protein-rich nut butters for spreads and for stuffing vegetables.

Bon appetit!

CARAWAY BLUE CHEESE WAFERS

1-1/4 c wholewheat pastry flour
1/3 c (2 oz) Blue cheese
1 T caraway seeds
1-1/4 c butter
1 T ice water

In a bowl combine flour, butter, cheese, and seeds, mixing until dough resembles coarse crumbs. Stir in 1 T ice water. With your hands, form dough into a roll about 1-1/2 inches in diameter. Wrap in foil and refrigerate overnight or until firm. Cut into 1/8 inch thick slices. Place on cookie sheet and sprinkle additional caraway seeds on top. Bake at 400° for 10 minutes. Serve warm or cold on a plate garnished with clusters of grapes. These wafers also make a tasty accompaniment for a simple soup or as a last course served with nuts and fresh fruit.

 **CHEESE BALLS**

1/2 c grated natural Cheddar cheese
2 T butter
1/2 c wholewheat pastry flour
1/4 c dried milk powder
1/4 t sea salt
1/4 t curry powder
dash of paprika

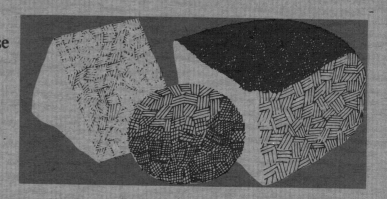

Cream cheese and butter together. Sift flour with powdered milk, salt, and curry. Gradually stir the flour mixture into the creamed cheese and butter, blending until mixed. With hands, take about a teaspoon of dough, forming it into a ball about the size of a marble. Place balls on ungreased baking sheet and flatten each with tines of a fork in a crisscross design. Sprinkle with paprika. Bake in a 450° oven for about 10 minutes. (Optional: before baking, sprinkle flattened balls with toasted sesame seeds.)

CRAB GELATIN CANAPES

2 T agar-agar flakes or unflavored gelatin
1/3 c sherry
1 c mayonnaise
1/2 t cayenne
1 T lemon juice
1/2 c yogurt
1 c fresh crab, flaked

Soften agar-agar flakes in sherry for 5 minutes, then dissolve in top of double boiler over hot water. When cool, add mayonnaise, cayenne, and lemon juice. Stir thoroughly. Then stir in yogurt, adding salt and pepper to taste.

Chill mixture until it begins to thicken, then add crab. Spoon mixture into a 2-1/2 cup mold which has been lightly oiled. Chill several hours or overnight. Unmold on a serving tray and circle with rye crackers.

EGG FOO YONG CANAPES

6 eggs, beaten
2 T chives, minced
1 green pepper, minced
1/2 c celery, chopped
1 T tamari
2 c mung bean sprouts, chopped
1/2 c mushrooms, chopped
peanut oil

Beat eggs, then stir in other ingredients except peanut oil.

Using two six-compartment muffin tins, fill bottom of each compartment with one-fourth inch of oil. Divide the mixture between these 12 compartments.

Bake in a 400° oven for about 10 minutes, or until gold brown. Run a knife around edges of each compartment and gently lift out the individual egg foo yong, setting on a paper towel to absorb excess oil. Serve on rounds of toasted wholewheat bread. Makes 12.

MUSHROOM CANAPES

1/2 lb mushrooms, minced
3 T corn germ oil
3 T wholewheat flour
1 c milk
1/4 c powdered milk
1/4 t sea salt

dash paprika
dash nutmeg
1/4 c yogurt
24 toasted wholewheat bread rounds
parsley

Saute minced mushrooms.

Prepare cream sauce by heating oil and blending in flour, stirring for 5 minutes. Then add milk pre-mixed with powdered milk. Cook and stir sauce with wire whisk until thickened. Add salt, paprika and nutmeg. When cold, stir in yogurt and pour over mushrooms. Serve cold in a bowl garnished with parsley and circled by bread rounds.

GREEN GODDESS DIP

2 soft avocados, mashed
1 c yogurt
1/4 c Tofu mayonnaise
1 T lemon juice
parsley
chives
1 t tamari
1/4 dried dill

Add yogurt to mashed avocado, then blend in mayonnaise and lemon juice. Mix in remaining ingredients, blending until light and fluffy. Chill for 1 hour. Serve in scooped out avocado shells surrounded with wholewheat crackers and a variety of raw vegetables prepared for dipping.

COCKTAIL MEATBALLS

1/4 c milk
2 T powdered milk
1 lb ground beef chuck
1/2 c dry wholewheat bread crumbs
1/4 c Burgundy wine
1/4 c green onions, finely chopped
1 t dried marjoram

1/4 t ground thyme
1 t sea salt
1/4 c corn germ oil
1 c bouillon
2 tomatoes, pureed
2 c yogurt

Blend together the milk and powdered milk.

Combine meat, bread crumbs, wine, milk, onions, seasonings, and shape into bite-sized meatballs. Cover and refrigerate until ready to use.

Saute meatballs in oil until browned. Place in chafing dish.

Combine bouillon and tomato puree and bring to a boil. Remove from heat. Stir in yogurt. Pour mixture over meatballs. Serve in chafing dish, with toothpicks readily available.

 ## SHRIMP DIP

1/4 lb mushrooms, sliced
2 T butter
1-1/2 c cottage cheese
2 T olive oil
2 T lemon juice
1/2 t sea salt
1/4 t garlic salt
1/4 t tamari
1/3 lb shrimp, cooked and minced
1/4 c yogurt

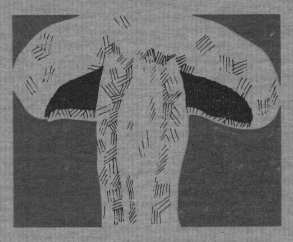

Saute mushrooms in butter. Add cottage cheese, oil, lemon juice, garlic salt, salt, and tamari; stir, then add shrimp. Simmer until hot. Remove from heat and stir in yogurt. Serve warm in a bowl placed in the center of a tray of rye wafers. Garnish tray with cherry tomatoes and bouquets of parsley.

SHRIMP HORS D'OEUVRES

1 lb shrimp
3 Bermuda onions, sliced thin
1/2 c lemon juice
2 t tamari
1 t honey

1/4 t ginger
1 bay leaf
1/4 c peanut oil
1/4 t dill

Cook shrimp in the usual way, or blanch shrimp for two minutes in strong sassafras tea. Remove shells and devein.

Combine all ingredients, except onions and shrimp, in a saucepan. Bring to a boil. Lower heat and simmer for five minutes, then add shrimp and cook 2 minutes more.

Place a layer of onion slices in a casserole, then cover with a layer of shrimp; repeat, ending with a top layer of onions. Pour the liquid over the shrimp and onions. Cover and place in refrigerator for two days.

Serve the shrimp with toothpicks for spearing; circle with rounds of rye on which you have placed the drained onion slices.

Soups

Served piping hot in cool or cold weather, or chilled in warm or hot weather, soups make a nice beginning for any nutritious meal.

Soup is relatively quick and easy, especially when you've planned ahead by stocking up on stock. With stock in your refrigerator your soup can often be on the table quickly while the rest of the dinner cooks.

Vegetable stock and other natural foods turn your soup pot into a primary source of good nutrition. Whether your soup is just the beginning, or the meal's principal dish, keep in mind the opportunities for even more natural food nutrition — as you take the soup off the fire, add a handful of vitamin-rich sprouted seeds, beans, or grain. Sprouted rye adds a flavor much like wild rice. Alfalfa sprouts lend freshness and wheat sprouts add sweetness.

Add two tablespoons of miso to thicken it. If the other flavors in the soup are fairly definite you can also add two or three tablespoons of nutritional yeast just before serving. For more protein, stir in a half cup of softened soy grits to a bean or cream soup. Into your creamed soups blend powdered milk.

23

Garnish with yogurt and serve with croutons you make yourself.

Soup making can be as creative as it is worthwhile nutritionally. Use imagination in adding herbs and seasonings as well as grains, nuts and wine. Use your head and your heart.

BULGARIAN BORSCHT

2 T corn germ oil
2 onions, chopped
4 beets, grated
1 carrot, grated
4 c beet water and stock

1 head cabbage, shredded
1/2 t dill
1 t vege-salt
2 T miso
1/2 c yogurt

Saute onions in oil until golden, then add beets and carrots, cooking lightly. Combine with stock in a covered saucepan and simmer for 15 minutes. Add cabbage, cooking until tender or about 10 minutes. Add dill, salt, and miso. Remove from heat and stir in yogurt.

Serve hot or cold with rye bread and butter, sliced apples, and cheese.

Serves 6.

25

 **MINESTRONE**

1/2 c kidney beans	2 quarts stock
1/4 c olive oil	1/2 c wholewheat macaroni
1 clove garlic	2 t tamari
1 onion, sliced	1/2 t rosemary
2 zucchini, diced	1/2 t basil
1 stalk broccoli, diced	3 T nutritional yeast
2 carrots, diced	2 T parsley
2 tomatoes, pureed	1/4 c Parmesan cheese, grated

Soak beans overnight. Add beans to 1 cup of boiling water, reducing heat immediately. Simmer until almost tender, 2 to 2-1/2 hours. Drain.

Saute garlic, onion, fresh zucchini, broccoli, and carrots in oil for 5 minutes; add pureed tomatoes. Whirl cooked beans in blender or press through sieve and add to stock, cooking 25 minutes. Add sauteed vegetables, macaroni, seasoning, nutritional yeast, and cook 15 minutes longer, or until macaroni is tender. Sprinkle soup with Parmesan cheese and add parsley. Serves 6.

 GAZPACHO (cold Spanish soup)

1 large tomato, chopped
1 cucumber, sliced and chopped
1 green pepper, chopped
1 onion, minced
1 clove garlic, minced
1/2 t vege-salt

1 t paprika
1 c homemade tomato juice
2 T olive oil
2 T lemon juice
1/2 c white wine

Peel tomato and cucumber; remove seeds from green pepper. Chop vegetables, then put into blender with minced onion, garlic, salt, paprika, and tomato juice. Blend at high speed. Add oil and lemon. Chill for two hours.

At serving time, add wine and several ice cubes. Pour into soup tureen and set on platter where you've arranged bowls of condiments to be used as garnish. Include among the condiments: chopped hard-cooked eggs, sliced ripe olives, sliced pimientos, cucumber slices, and alfalfa sprouts. Serve gazpacho with rye bread spread with garlic butter and toasted under the broiler. Serves 4.

CHERRY-WINE SOUP

2 lb red cherries, pitted,
    or use soaked dried cherries
2 c water
cinnamon stick
2 whole cloves
2 drops almond extract

1/4 t sea salt
2 c red wine
4 t arrowroot
6 T cold water
honey to taste

Simmer cherries in water with seasonings until soft. Press through sieve or whirl in blender. Add wine and honey to taste.

Place over heat; when hot, add arrowroot blended with cold water to a smooth consistency.

Cook slowly, stirring constantly until clear. Serve ice-cold with dab of yogurt, or serve hot as a dessert with cookies. Serves 6.

CREAM OF CHESTNUT SOUP

2 c dry chestnuts
2 c stock
1 stalk celery, diced
2 c hot milk
1/2 c powdered milk
3 T nutritional yeast

2 T butter
2 T wholewheat flour
1 onion, minced
dash of paprika
pinch of nutmeg

Soak dried chestnuts overnight. Drain, peel, and boil in stock with celery until soft. Press chestnuts thru a sieve or whirl in blender until pureed.

Blend milk with powdered milk and nutritional yeast, then combine with chestnut puree.

Saute onions in butter, add flour, and stir until blended.

Combine onion-flour mixture with liquid mixture and simmer for 10 minutes.

Sprinkle with paprika and a dash of nutmeg. Serves 4.

2 cucumbers, unpeeled and sliced
1 onion, sliced
1 small potato, diced
1 c stock
2 c yogurt

1 t dill
1 clove garlic
3 T nutritional yeast
3 T peanut oil
1 T mint, crushed

Place cucumbers, onion and potato in a saucepan with stock and cook for 10 minutes until vegetables are almost soft. Add 1 cup cold water. When mixture is cool, pour off liquid and put vegetables in blender with yogurt, dill, garlic, nutritional yeast, oil, and mint leaves. Blend until smooth.

Chill and serve with a dab of yogurt and fresh mint leaves. The soup makes a nice accompaniment to a fruit or vegetable salad and a hearty dessert. Serves 4.

CHEDDAR CHEESE SOUP

1/2 c carrots, grated
1/2 c celery, chopped
3 c stock
1 onion, chopped
1/4 c corn germ oil
3 T wholewheat flour
2 c milk

1/2 c powdered milk
3 T nutritional yeast
1/2 lb Cheddar cheese, grated
1/2 c yogurt
1/2 t celery seed
dash paprika

Cook carrots and celery in one cup stock until tender. Saute onion in oil, stirring in flour until blended.

In the blender combine milk, powdered milk, and nutritional yeast with 2 cups of stock. Gradually add this milk mixture to the onion mixture, stirring over low heat until thick.

Add cheese and vegetables. Remove from heat and stir in yogurt and celery seed. Sprinkle with paprika. Serves 6.

3 onions, sliced
2 T butter
2 T wholewheat flour
3 c stock
1 c white wine
6 slices wholewheat bread, dried
1/4 lb Swiss cheese, grated
1/4 lb Swiss cheese, sliced

Using a heavy skillet, cook onions in butter for about 10 minutes or until slightly browned. Sprinkle with wholewheat flour and cook 2 minutes more. Add stock and simmer 15 minutes longer. Pour ingredients into a casserole. Add wine. Place bread slices on top of liquid, then top bread with the grated and sliced cheese. Heat in a 450° degree oven for 10 minutes. Serves 6.

 **BEAN SOUP**

1 onion
2 T butter
3 T nutritional yeast
3/4 lb white dried beans, soaked overnight
6 c stock
2 carrots, sliced

1 bay leaf
1/2 t thyme
2 celery stalks, sliced
1 t sea salt
1/2 c burgundy

Saute sliced onion in butter for 5 minutes, or until soft. Add nutritional yeast, beans, stock, vegetables, and seasonings. Bring to a boil, then cover and simmer for two hours or until beans are very tender.

Drain beans and vegetables, reserving the liquid, and mash all ingredients. Stir in the retained liquid and return to pan. Add wine, heating for two minutes. Remove from heat and add 2 tablespoons of butter cut into small pieces.

Serve with croutons. Serves 4.

1 onion, minced
1/4 c corn germ oil
1/4 t caraway seeds
1-1/2 c fresh corn, cut from 3-4 ears
1-1/2 t sea salt
1/2 c stock

1-1/2 c milk
1/2 c powdered milk
1 T wholewheat flour
3 T nutritional yeast
1/4 c walnuts, ground

Saute onion in corn germ oil until soft, then add caraway seeds, corn, salt, and stock. Simmer for 10 minutes.

In another saucepan combine milk with powdered milk and yeast, heating to a boil.

Brown flour in a little butter and slowly add to milk mixture. Combine the milk and corn mixtures, cooking 5 minutes longer.

Garnish with walnuts. Serves 4.

Egg & Cheese Dishes

Eggs, cheese, milk — these simple ingredients when combined with skill can emerge as triumphs. A perfect omelet, a light and fluffy souffle, a savory quiche offer you vast opportunities for creativity.

When you use natural food counterparts you not only greatly increase nutritional values, but you serve glowing health and happiness in your omelets, souffles, and quiches.

Begin with fresh fertile eggs, natural cheeses and spray-dried non-instant milk and you are into natural foods.

Always insist on fertile eggs, for sale in natural food stores. These eggs, laid by chickens that have not been force-fed or filled with steroids and antibiotics, rate high nutritionally. They are rich in enzymes, estrogenic hormones and lecithin, the substance which helps humans use cholesterol properly. Because most fertile eggs come from local farmers, they are usually fresh — and fresh eggs make all the difference in the lightness and flavor of your egg dishes.

Just as you go to a little extra trouble to find a ready source of fertile eggs, seek out and use only natural cheeses instead of the mass produced and mass consumed processed cheeses.

Commercially processed cheeses are made solid by the mechanical process of hydrogenation and can contain as many as 31 additives, none of which is particularly good for you. Natural cheeses solidify because of a high concentration of milk protein and not because of the presence of foreign chemicals.

No dyes are added in making natural cheeses bright orange or bright yellow. Nor do the natural cheeses contain chemicals to prevent them from moulding so you do have to keep them carefully refrigerated.

To add more goodness to your egg and cheese dishes, fortify recipes requiring milk with extra powdered milk. Use spray-dried, non-instant powdered milk which has been separated from whole milk without the use of heat. By adding a fourth of a cup to your dishes, you double the calcium and protein content without altering the taste or consistency. Just half a cup of spray-dried, non-instant powdered milk equals a quart of regular liquid milk.

Buy yogurt and cottage cheese, often used in egg and cheese dishes, from a natural food store. Only then can you be sure they are pure and free of additives.

To enhance further the nutrition and flavor of your omelets, souffles and other egg-cheese dishes add poppy and sesame seeds — or sprinkle ground nuts or sunflower seeds in waffle and pancake batter for a new flavor and texture. As an inexpensive garnish, saute alfalfa sprouts with chives and herbs in butter and use as a topping for almost any dish.

 ## SPANISH OMELET

1/2 c peanut oil
3 T green pepper, chopped
3 T onion, chopped
4 T tomatoes, diced
4 T alfalfa sprouts
5 eggs
5 T milk
1/2 t sea salt
cayenne

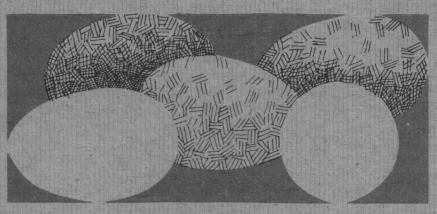

Prepare omelet filling before starting eggs: Heat oil in skillet and saute peppers and onions. Add tomatoes and sprouts, cooking until soft. Remove from heat.

Choose a pan with sloping sides, a flat bottom and smooth surface. Melt enough butter to form a thin layer over entire surface.

Beat eggs just enough to mix whites and yolks and then beat in the milk, salt, and cayenne. Pour egg mixture into heated pan; cook slowly. As mixture cooks, run spatula around the edge and lift omelet, tipping pan so uncooked portion will flow underneath. When mixture no longer flows, increase heat for a few seconds to brown bottom. Run spatula under omelet to loosen. Spread filling across center of omelet and fold one half of omelet over other half. Serve with Spaghetti Sauce (see page 69) and orange wedges. Serves 2 or more.

 PIZZA

2-1/2 c wholewheat flour
1-1/2 t dry yeast
2 t salt
1/4 c peanut oil
1/2 c milk

Soften yeast in three tablespoons of warm milk, about 85°. Let stand for 5 minutes, then mix in salt, oil, milk, and flour, beating with an electric mixer at low speed for one minute. Add enough flour to make a soft dough. Turn onto a lightly floured board and knead until smooth and elastic, about 10 minutes.

Place mixture in a greased bowl, turning dough to coat lightly with grease. Cover and let rise in a warm place until double in bulk, about 45 minutes. Punch dough down and divide into halves. Press dough into 2 greased 12-inch pans, forming rim. Use fingers to spread dough over the pan to about one-fourth inch thickness.

Cover pizza with 1 cup of onions that have been sauteed in 1/4 c oil, tomato sauce, and 1 t basil. Place anchovy fillets, mushrooms, olives, and peppers over onion mixture and sprinkle with grated Mozzarella or Jack cheese. Bake in 400° oven for 20 minutes.

Substitute other ingredients, experimenting with cooked aduki beans, carrots, zucchini, cauliflower, and different sauces, especially Bechamel Sauce. To make Bechamel Sauce, melt 2 T butter in a saucepan then add 2 T chopped onions, cooking until onions turn golden. Stir in 2 T wholewheat flour and 2-1/2 c hot milk. Stir until smooth. Add 1/2 t salt, 1/4 t pepper, and a pinch of grated nutmeg.

WAFFLES WITH SHERRY SAUCE

Waffles:

1 c wholewheat flour	1/2 c walnuts, ground	3 t corn germ oil
1 t sea salt	2 eggs, separated	2 T honey
1/2 c powdered milk	1/2 c yogurt	

Sift flour, salt and powdered milk. Stir in walnuts. Add yogurt, honey, oil and egg yolks. Beat egg whites and stir 1/3 into mixture; fold in the remaining portion. Bake waffles in iron, keeping cooked waffles warm in the oven.

Sherry Sauce:

1 T arrowroot	1/2 c Sherry	1 t lemon rind, grated
1 c honey	1 T lemon juice	1/2 c butter
1/2 c water		

Mix arrowroot with honey. Gradually add sherry and water, stirring smooth over heat. When mixture boils add lemon juice, rind and butter.

BAKED CHEESE FONDUE

6 slices wholewheat bread, cut in halves
softened butter
1-1/2 c (6 oz) natural Cheddar cheese, grated
3 eggs, beaten
1/2 t sea salt
cayenne
1 t chives, minced
3 c milk

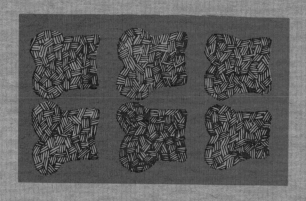

Spread bread with softened butter. Arrange on oiled baking dish. Sprinkle with cheese.

Mix eggs, salt, cayenne, chives, and milk. Pour over bread and let stand for 1 hour.

Bake in a 325° oven for 40 minutes. Serves 4-6.

1-1/2 c bouillon
6 T powdered milk
1/4 c wholewheat flour
1/2 t sea salt
2 T corn germ oil
1 T nutritional yeast

1 t parsley
1/2 t dill
1-1/2 t curry powder
6 hard cooked eggs, sliced
6 slices wholewheat toast, buttered

Blend all ingredients except eggs and bread. Turn into a saucepan and cook over gentle heat, stirring constantly until thickened and smooth.

Arrange the slices of egg on toast and pour the sauce on top. Serve with sauteed sprouts, mushrooms or peppers. Serves 6.

To hard-cook eggs: place eggs in cold water and bring just to a boil. Turn off heat; let stand covered for 15 minutes. Drain and replace hot water with cold. Remove shells as soon as eggs are cool enough to handle.

 QUICHE LORRAINE

Pastry:
1 T ice water
1/2 c corn germ oil
2 egg yolks
2 c wholewheat pastry flour

Make pastry dough by blending water, oil, yolks, and flour, adding a small amount of milk if necessary to make a stiff dough. Press into pie plate. Chill 1 hour.

Filling:
6 slices bacon (optional)
2 c heavy cream
1/2 c powdered milk
3 eggs
1/4 t sea salt

pinch nutmeg
1 t chopped chives
1/2 c natural Swiss cheese, grated
butter

Render bacon.

Combine eggs, cream, powdered milk, salt, and nutmeg in blender. Spread a little butter over the bottom of the pastry shell and then sprinkle first with crumbled bacon and then with cheese. Pour egg-milk mixture on top.

Bake in a 400° oven for 15 minutes; reduce heat to 300° and bake 15 minutes more. Let cool slightly, but serve warm. Serves 6.

In place of bacon and cheese use pureed vegetables, especially spinach and carrots with a dash of curry powder. For a Spanish style quiche, add sauteed green peppers, onions and pimentos and garnish with broiled tomatoes. Or serve a plain quiche without bacon or cheese and for enhancement, top with your favorite sauce.

# WELSH RAREBIT

2 T green pepper, chopped
2 t onion, chopped
1 clove garlic, minced
1 T corn germ oil
1 T butter
1 T wholewheat flour
1/4 t sea salt

1/3 c milk
2 T powdered milk
1 t chili powder
1/2 t ground cumin seed
1 c sharp Cheddar cheese, grated
7 slices rye toast

Saute peppers, onion and garlic in oil. Remove from pan. Melt butter then blend in flour, salt. Add milk and powdered milk, stirring until mixture thickens and comes to a boil. Remove from heat; stir in sauteed ingredients, seasonings, and cheese.

Spread on toasted rye bread and broil until lightly brown. Garnish with watercress that's been dipped momentarily in hot water. Serves 3-4.

RICOTTA PANCAKES

1 c Ricotta cheese
3 eggs
2 T sesame oil
1/4 c wholewheat flour
2 t honey

1/4 t sea salt
2 c fresh fruit, preferably berries
soft butter
date sugar

In blender combine ricotta, eggs, oil, flour, honey, and salt. Blend until smooth.

Pour batter on lightly oiled griddle or in frying pan over medium low heat, using enough batter to make 3-inch round cakes. Turn cakes with spatula when bubbles form on the surface. When cakes are browned on both sides, remove from pan and keep warm until all the cakes are cooked.

The ricotta cakes can be made ahead, cooled on wire racks, then reheated on baking sheets covered with foil in a 350° oven for 5 minutes.

Serve with berries warmed in a small amount of water with date sugar and salt.

SESAME SCRAMBLED EGGS

7 eggs
1/4 c milk
2 T milk powder
1/3 t sea salt
pepper
2 T butter
1-1/2 c yogurt
2 T toasted sesame seeds
1/2 t chervil

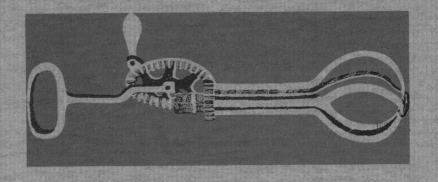

Combine eggs, milk, milk powder, salt, pepper, and beat with a rotary beater until frothy.

Heat butter in a large skillet. Pour egg mixture into skillet and cook over low heat until eggs are almost done — set, but still a little damp. Remove from heat and stir in yogurt, chervil, and sesame seeds. Serve with sauteed mushrooms, green peppers, or alfalfa sprouts. Serves 4.

CHEESE SOUFFLE

1-1/2 c milk	4 eggs, separated
1/4 c powdered milk	1/2 t thyme
3 T nutritional yeast	1 c natural Swiss cheese, grated
3 T wholewheat flour	1/2 c Parmesan cheese, grated
1-1/2 t sea salt	

Heat 1 cup milk in double boiler until it simmers. Meanwhile, in a blender mix the powdered milk, yeast, flour, and salt, with 1/2 c milk. Combine the two mixtures, and simmer for 5 minutes, stirring constantly. Remove from heat, cool slightly, then stir in beaten egg yolks, thyme and the cheeses.

Beat egg whites stiffly until shiny but not dry. Stir in one-third of the egg whites, then fold in remaining whites. Don't overmix; you should be able to see some of the whites. Pour mixture into greased souffle dish, or casserole with vertical sides. Run the tip of a spoon around the souffle an inch from the edge to make a slight depression. Bake at 300 for 45-60 minutes. Souffles are best right out of the oven, so have your guests seated and waiting. Serves 4-6.

Vegetable Entrees

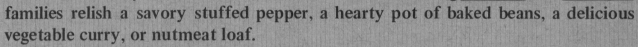

Even non-vegetarians enjoy meatless main dishes.

For variety in their diets, conventional meat-eating families relish a savory stuffed pepper, a hearty pot of baked beans, a delicious vegetable curry, or nutmeat loaf.

These protein-rich vegetable entrees provide not only a welcome change in flavor and texture from the usual meat entree, but also give the natural foods cook the opportunity to use some of the world's most nutritious foods.

Added to the tasty cheeses, nuts and beans at the base of many of these entrees, are such other natural foods as soybeans, wheat germ, sunflower seeds and nutritional yeast.

Many nutritionists believe that two-thirds of our daily diet should be composed of animal protein, so, if they are correct, the non-meat eater must make up for this lack with high quality vegetable proteins, eggs, and cheese. The soy bean, the only meatless source of complete protein, is an easy solution to the problem. Not only does the soy bean provide all needed amino acids, but this protein-storehouse is flavorless, which means it won't change the taste of your favorite dish.

For best results use soy beans in the form of soy grits — the bean cracked into 8 or 10 pieces. Grits don't have to be cooked like the whole bean which must be simmered for several hours. Instead, they are ready to use after only 15 minutes soaking time. Add a fourth of a cup of soy grits to almost any stuffing or loaf — an amount that is equivalent in protein to a half-pound of ground round or steak. When the soy grit complements other proteins like cheese, beans, and nuts, you'll be providing meals with more than adequate protein.

Both wheat germ and sunflower seeds also provide high proportions of protein. Use wheat germ in place of bread crumbs and as a tasty topping for most baked dishes, especially when combined with paprika and dotted with butter. Use sunflower seeds in just about anything — as a crunchy topping for a loaf, or ground and used as stuffing for tomatoes, peppers, or mixed into loaves.

Nutritional yeast or brewers yeast ranks as the highest source of protein known — just one heaping tablespoonful provides as much protein as a serving of meat. So even the addition of 1 or 2 tablespoons to entrees can do a great deal in providing hard-to-get protein. Be sure you buy the mild flavored kind (see Stock Your Shelves, page xii), use a small amount at first, and use the yeast only in recipes with an herb or seasoning to mask the flavor.

Probably no other category of food preparation offers a greater opportunity to join the league of "THE WISE COOK" — you who want the best possible nutrition for your loved ones. These wise cooks, already at work across the country, know that what can't be tasted can't be complained about. Only "THE WISE COOK" knows that within that delicious casserole hides a protein-heavy helping of soy grits, wheat germ, or nutritional yeast — maybe even all three!

You're the same artful cook who answers the question: "Mom, how come your stuff tastes so much better than anyone elses?" by simply smiling and replying softly: "Because I put lots of love in my cooking, dear."

NUT STUFFED CABBAGE

1 head cabbage
1/2 c wholewheat bread crumbs (2 pieces of toast)
1 t poultry seasoning
1 onion, chopped
1/2 c soy grits, softened in 1 c water for 15 minutes

1 c cashews, chopped
1/2 c celery, diced
4 tomatoes, pureed
1 c bouillon
1/2 t oregano

Parboil cabbage by covering with boiling water and letting stand for 5 minutes. Remove the cabbage, return 12 outer leaves to pot, cover again with boiling water, let stand covered for another 5 minutes. Remove from water, drain. Grate remainder of cabbage and place in bottom of a casserole. Mix bread crumbs with poultry seasoning. Saute onion. Combine onion, bread crumbs, then add nuts, soy grits and celery.

Divide mixture onto the 12 cabbage leaves. Fold, then roll up like cigar and tie with string. Place fold side down in casserole. Pour pureed tomatoes and bouillon mixed with oregano over the rolls. Bake at 375° for one hour. Serves 6.

Garnish rolls with a dab of yogurt.

STUFFED PEPPERS

4 green peppers
1 c lentils, cooked
1/2 c natural Cheddar cheese, grated
3 T nutritional yeast
1/2 t thyme

1 onion, chopped
2 T corn germ oil
2 T wheat germ
paprika

Cut peppers in half lengthwise, remove seeds and fibers then cover with boiling water. Let stand off heat 10-15 minutes. Drain.

Saute onions in oil. Combine with other ingredients except wheat germ and paprika. Stuff peppers. Top with sprinkling of wheat germ and paprika.

Let stand in refrigerator for several hours to improve flavor.

Place peppers in a casserole, add a little water and bake at 350° for 20-30 minutes. For perfect peppers, insert a meat thermometer for a moment after 20 minutes of cooking and if temperature registers 140°-150°, peppers are just right.

Serve peppers with a corn or chestnut soup, a baked yellow squash, and molded fruit salad.

 BAKED BEANS

1-1/2 c kidney or soy beans,
     soaked overnight
2 c water
2 c apple juice
2 T dark molasses
tomato, diced

1 T dry mustard
1 t vege salt
1/2 c boiling bean stock
1/2 t vinegar
1 t curry powder

Bring apple juice and water to a boil and add beans so slowly that boiling doesn't stop. Reduce heat after beans are in water and simmer 2-2-1/2 hours or until beans are almost tender. Drain beans, reserving liquid, and add other ingredients to beans. Place in oiled baking dish and bake covered 2-3 hours in a 250° oven. Uncover for the last hour of cooking. If beans become dry, add a little of the reserved bean water. About 15 minutes before removing from the oven add the fresh diced tomato. Serves 6. Serve with cottage cheese and fruit salad, a green vegetable, and wholewheat crackers.

STUFFED EGGPLANT

3 small eggplants
1 T sesame seeds
3 medium onions, chopped
1 green pepper, chopped
1/2 c celery, diced
1/2 c sesame oil

2 tomatoes, chopped
1 t sesame salt
1/2 t bay leaf
pinch of cloves, cayenne
1/2 c soy grits, soaked in 1 c water for 15 minutes
1/2 c natural Swiss cheese, grated

Cut eggplant lengthwise and remove thin slice from the bottom of each half so vegetable will sit securely in pan. Scoop out insides, leaving a quarter inch shell. Cover eggplant with boiling water in which salt has been added and bring again to a boil, then turn off heat and let stand 5 minutes before removing from the water.

Saute sesame seeds, onion, pepper, and celery in oil. Add tomatoes, 1 t salt, seasonings, and part of the scooped-out eggplant pulp (discard the seedier portion). Simmer 10 minutes. Combine with soy grits and spoon into eggplant shells. Top with cheese and dot with butter. Bake at 350° for 1 hour. Serves 6.

STUFFED BAKED TOMATOES

6 firm tomatoes
1/2 lb walnuts or cashews, ground
1/2 c soy grits, softened in 1 c water
1/4 c Cheddar cheese, grated
1/4 c green pepper, chopped
1/4 c sprouts, chopped
1/3 c stock
1/4 t sea salt
1 T olive oil

Core tomatoes and gently scoop out the pulp. Dice pulp and mix with other ingredients. Stuff mixture gently into tomatoes.

Pour oil in the bottom of a casserole and arrange tomatoes in dish. Bake at 350° for 30 minutes. The tomatoes will make their own sauce while baking. Serve with a hearty soup, a fruit salad, crackers, and cheese. Serves 4-6.

 CURRY

1 apple, finely chopped
1 onion, finely chopped
3 T corn germ oil
1 T wholewheat flour
1 T curry powder
1 c cream

Saute apple and onion over low heat in oil until soft but not brown.

Mix in flour and curry powder. Add cream and stir until thickened.

Serve over long grain brown rice or over vegetables and garbanzo beans. Serve some or all of the following condiments which each guest can add himself: raisins and mangoes, peanuts, sprouted fenugreek seeds, hard cooked eggs, grated fresh coconut, toasted sunflower seeds, fennel seeds, or sesame seeds.

For those who don't like their curry hot, serve a bowl of yogurt to cool things down. Serves 4-6.

COTTAGE CHEESE NUTLOAF

2 c cottage cheese
2 c walnuts, chopped
1/2 c bread or cracker crumbs
1/2 c soy grits, soaked in 1 cup water for 15 minutes
1 onion, minced
2 tomatoes, pureed
2 T lemon juice
2 T peanut oil

Mix all ingredients and put in 12x9x2 inch pan. Bake at 350° for 30-40 minutes. Serve hot with a cream sauce or use cold as a sandwich filling. Serves 4-6.

SPICED AVOCADOS OVER RICE

2 onions, chopped
1 clove garlic
2 large green peppers, minced
2 small hot red peppers
1/4 c olive oil
1/4 c pureed fresh tomatoes
1/2 c vinegar
1 t sea salt
3 large avocados, minced
1/2 lb fried bacon, crumbled (optional)
4 c cooked brown rice

Cook onions, garlic and peppers in hot oil until onions are golden then add tomatoe puree, vinegar and salt. Simmer mixture for 30 minutes. Cook slightly and stir in avocados and bacon. Serve over brown rice. Serves 8.

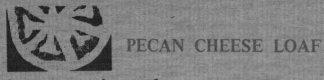

PECAN CHEESE LOAF

1 c pecans, chopped
1 c natural Cheddar cheese, grated
1/2 c wholewheat germ
1/4 c soy grits, soaked in 1/2 c stock for 15 minutes
3/4 t sea salt
1/2 t paprika
1 T onion, grated
1 T parsley, minced
2 eggs, beaten

Combine all ingredients except wheat germ. After well mixed, then stir in the wheat germ. Turn into loaf pan. Bake at 350° for 30 minutes. Serves 6.

Serve with mushroom sauce made by sauteing 1/4 pound mushroom caps in 2 tablespoons corn germ oil and then adding 2 tablespoons wholewheat flour, 1/2 teaspoon salt, dash of nutmeg and a half cup each of milk and cream. Cook until smooth and thick.

WALNUTMEAT SPAGHETTI

2 T sesame oil
1 large onion, chopped
1/2 green pepper, chopped
1 clove garlic, minced
4 c tomatoes, peeled and diced
1 T pimiento, chopped
2 t honey

1 t vege-salt
1/4 t basil
1/4 t oregano
1/4 c miso
1/2 lb black walnuts, chopped
8 oz wholewheat spaghetti

Saute onions, pepper, garlic in oil. Add seasonings, tomatoes, pimientos, honey, and salt. Bring to a boil, then simmer covered for 20 minutes. Add miso and walnuts. Take off heat, cool and refrigerate for 4 hours to improve flavor.

Twenty minutes before serving time, bring 2 quarts of water to a boil and add spaghetti slowly so boiling does not stop. Add a tablespoon of oil and 2 teaspoons salt to the water. Cook from 10 to 15 minutes or until tender.

Meanwhile reheat the spaghetti sauce. Serve with a green vegetable and a fruit salad. Serves 4.

69

Vegetables

As a creative cook you can use your basket of fresh vegetables — purple-black eggplant, shiny red tomatoes, golden carrots, pale green lettuce, rich green spinach and mustard leaves — as the painter uses his palette.

Sometimes serve these beautiful raw materials just as they are or lightly cooked with butter and seasonings. At other times you'll use flourishes that transform simple vegetables into gourmet fare.

However you serve them, vegetables lend both color and texture contrast to your meals. With white fish, spinach and tomatoes add color contrast, while the paleness of cooked eggplant and mushrooms complement red meat. The crunchiness of lightly cooked broccoli or carrots goes well with the softness of meat loaf while the soft texture of potatoes and squash goes better with a chewy entree.

Vegetables also provide vitamins, minerals and enzymes to be obtained in no other food — especially organically grown vegetables. Nurtured in chemical-free soil, these contain only the minerals which nature put into the soil. These absorbed minerals then find their way into our own bodies.

To retain the best flavor, take care in the preparation, storage and cooking of your vegetables. Oxidation kills vitamins so don't leave vegetables exposed to air, refrigerate them instead. Wash just before cooking and pop them into steaming kettles filled with small amounts of water. Save the leftover water for stock since it contains an abundance of water-soluble vitamins. Better yet, cook your vegetables in milk, wine, beer, or oil and use the cooking liquid as a sauce.

For those times when you want to serve a glamorous vegetable dish, substitute sea salt or sesame salt for the salt called for in standard recipes. Instead of using butter for vegetable cookery try corn germ oil. Use honey in place of sugar, wholewheat bread crumbs in place of white bread crumbs, yogurt instead of sour cream.

The recipes that follow illustrate these points and suggest new ideas about seasonings plus unusual additions that you can adapt to your own favorite vegetable recipes.

1-3/4 c water
2 c peas
2 T corn germ oil
1 onion, chopped
1/4 head of lettuce, finely shredded
2 t honey
salt
1 t wholewheat flour
1 small avocado, cut into 8 thick slices

Add peas to 1-1/4 cup boiling water and cook for 2 minutes. Drain. Heat 1 T oil in saucepan, add onion and lettuce, and cook until soft. Add peas, 1/2 c boiling water, honey, salt. Combine flour with 1 T oil, making a smooth paste, then add to peas. Pour mixture into casserole. Arrange avocado slices on top. Cover and bake at 425° for 12 minutes. Serves 4.

ORIENTAL CARROTS

1 small onion, chopped
1 T sesame oil
2 t curry powder
3 c carrots, cooked
2 t cider vinegar
1-1/2 t vege-salt
1/2 c coconut, grated

Saute onion in oil. Add curry powder, then carrots, vinegar, and salt. Cook until carrots are hot. Serve with freshly grated coconut. Serves 6.

HONEY GLAZED ONIONS

2 Spanish onions
4 whole cloves
1 T honey
1 t sesame salt
dash nutmeg, cayenne
2 T corn germ oil
3 T toasted almonds, slivered

Place peeled and halved onions in 2 inches of boiling salted water. Bring to boil again, then cover and simmer for 20 minutes or until almost tender. Drain water off onions. Place a whole clove in each onion half. Put onions in a casserole.

Mix together the honey, salt, nutmeg, cayenne, and corn germ oil and pour over onions. Cover casserole and bake in a 300° oven for 45 minutes, occasionally using the glaze from the bottom of the casserole for basting.

Sprinkle with almonds at serving time. Serves 4.

BAKED POTATO AU GRATIN

4 baked potatoes
1/2 t sea salt
1/2 c natural Cheddar cheese, grated
1/4 c green peppers, diced
2 T pimientos, diced
1 c yogurt
1/4 c wholewheat bread crumbs (one slice of toasted bread)

Wash and scrub even-sized Idaho potatoes. Bake for 40 minutes in 425° oven. When half done, pull out rack and quickly puncture skin to permit steam to escape. Return to oven to finish baking. When done, cut lengthwise into halves. Remove pulp without breaking skin. Mash pulp and combine with other ingredients except bread crumbs.

Cover filled potato shells with bread crumbs. Place under the broiler for a few moments until golden brown crust forms. Serves 4.

APPLES AND SAUERKRAUT

2 T corn germ oil
1 medium onion, chopped
2 apples, cored and sliced
2 c sauerkraut, cooked for 1 hour in 1/2 cup water
1 T caraway seeds
1/3 c yogurt

Saute onions and apple in oil. Add sauerkraut with cooking liquid and caraway. Cook covered 1 hour. Drain off liquid. Stir in yogurt. Serves 6.

RED CABBAGE WITH VERMOUTH

1 small red cabbage
2 T corn germ oil
1/2 c onion, diced
7 T sweet vermouth
1 T honey
3/4 t sesame salt
1-1/2 c seedless white grapes, cut in half
1 t lemon juice
1 t arrowroot

Remove outside leaves of cabbage and shred coarsely.

Saute onion in oil until limp. Add cabbage, 4 T of vermouth, honey and salt. Mix lightly. Cover and cook for 8 minutes or until cabbage is barely tender.

Add grapes and lemon juice. Cover and cook for one minute. Blend arrowroot with remaining vermouth and add to cabbage. Cook until juice thickens slightly. Serves 4.

STUFFED MUSHROOMS

12 large mushrooms
1 c wholewheat bread crumbs
1/4 c walnuts, chopped
2 ripe tomatoes, pureed
1/4 t rosemary
2 T parsley, chopped

Remove mushroom stems, wash and dry caps.

Mix bread crumbs with walnuts, tomato puree, rosemary and parsley.

Stuff mushrooms and place in a baking dish. Top each with a little sesame oil and salt. Bake at 375° for 15 minutes or until tender. Serves 4.

APPLES, CARROTS, BEETS

1 medium onion, chopped
1/2 c corn germ oil
1 large apple, peeled and diced
4 medium carrots, thinly sliced
1 small bunch of beets, cooked and diced
1/4 t nutmeg

Brown onion in oil and add apples, beets and carrots. Season with nutmeg, salt and pepper. Cover and simmer gently for about 20 minutes or until tender. Serves 6.

 **CREAMED SPINACH**

2 c spinach, cooked
2 T corn germ oil
2 T wholewheat flour
1/2 c cream, heated

Puree cooked spinach in blender. Heat oil in skillet, stir in flour and then cream. When sauce is smooth add the cooked spinach. Cook for 3 minutes. Season with a dash of nutmeg. Serves 4.

SUMMER SQUASH WITH GREEN BEANS

2 young summer squash
1 lb green beans
2 T butter
2 T almonds, slivered

Slice squash in half lengthwise. Brush cut sides with oil and lay on baking sheet. Bake in 375° oven for about 20 minutes or until tender.

Meanwhile, wash the beans, setting large ones aside for later use in a soup or stew. Leave the small ones whole and slice the medium sized ones.

Add beans to 2 quarts boiling water and cook uncovered for 15 minutes. Drain. Turn beans into a skillet, shaking them over heat until all moisture has evaporated. When dry, add butter to skillet and shake pan until butter has melted and coats beans.

Fill cooked squash with green beans and sprinkle almonds on top. Serves 4.

Fish & Chicken

Both fish and chicken rank high in protein, and both cost less per serving than most meats. Besides, fish and chicken offer you the perfect background for your special sauce — whether it be a delicate creamy topping fragrant with herbs, or a zestful one replete with onions and garlic.

And fish ranks as one of our most wholesome foods. Except for the hazards of water pollution, little can be done to alter the high natural nutrition and goodness of freshly caught fish. The trick is locating really fresh fish; you can always tell a fresh fish by sniffing — no smell and it's fresh. One answer to finding fresh fish is to find first a small market where the butcher will honestly tell you which fish is the freshest. Then, with knowing preparation, any fish will taste delicious.

Wash the fish quickly just before cooking and dry it immediately so moisture doesn't wash away flavorful juices and vitamins. Because fish has much less fat than meat, heat penetrates more rapidly so it cooks faster. The only way you can ruin fish is by overcooking it. For best results use a thermometer for oven cooking and remove the fish when the heat registers 145°-150°. Salt the fish when it's served, not before.

Since most chickens on the market have been fed synthetic food, pumped full of chemicals and raised in artificial environments, locating a wholesome specimen becomes difficult. Fortunately, many natural food stores now offer organically-raised chickens — chickens that have been free to exercise, to peck in the dirt, and to find the foods nature intended them to have. These chickens, raised for their maximum nutritive qualities and not just the weight and size, offer more vitamins and are also free of the chemical residue found in non-organic chickens.

To bring out the finest flavors and to assure getting enough unsaturated fatty acid in your diet, cook both chicken and fish in unrefined vegetable oils — one of the natural food advocate's most important foods.

For further nutritional benefit, add one teaspoon of kelp to your seafood dishes and nutritional yeast to both fish and chicken dishes. Use wheat germ as a dip for both before frying or use a mixture of wholewheat flour, milk powder and an herb such as basil, tarragon or dill.

Serve fresh fish and organically-raised chicken often. Whether presented plain or enhanced with that perfect sauce, they offer good, inexpensive eating.

FILLET OF SOLE FLORENTINE

6 fillets of sole　　　　　dry bread crumbs
1-1/2 c creamed spinach　　butter

Poach fillets in 1-1/2 c water (or 1/2 water, 1/2 white wine). Bring almost to simmer and maintain for 8-12 minutes. Arrange poached, drained fillets over creamed spinach, cover with white sauce, sprinkle with bread crumbs, dot with butter and put under broiler to heat through.

Sauce:
2 T corn germ oil　　　　1 egg yolk
1 T wholewheat flour　　　2 T lemon juice
2 c water　　　　　　　　1 t kelp
1/2 t salt

Mix flour with hot oil, add water, salt, yolk, stir briskly over low flame. Remove just before boiling point, add lemon juice and kelp.

SHRIMP NEWBURG

1/2 c sesame oil
1 t chives, chopped
1/4 c sherry
1 c yogurt
3 egg yolks, beaten
1 lb shrimp, cooked
1 c long-grain brown rice, cooked

Heat oil in a heavy saucepan, adding chives and wine, cooking for about 3 minutes. In a bowl blend egg yolks and yogurt then add to saucepan mixture, stirring constantly until sauce thickens. Add shrimp and pour over rice. Serves 4.

POACHED FISH STEAK WITH ANCHOVY SAUCE

3 lb halibut	8 peppercorns	1 T lemon juice
1-1/2 c beer	1 bay leaf	

Cut halibut into suitable servings. Cover in skillet with boiling beer. Add peppercorns, bay leaf, and lemon juice and simmer for about 10 minutes.

Sauce:

2 T corn germ oil	small onion, chopped	3 fillets of anchovy
2 T wholewheat flour	cloves	onion rings
1 c milk	bay leaf	

Serve with Anchovy Sauce: Heat oil in saucepan then add flour, blending well, and cook for 5 minutes over low heat. Slowly add milk and cook until thickened. Add onion, cloves and bay leaf and place in a 350° oven for 20 minutes. Remove from oven and add the anchovy fillets which have been pureed in your blender. Place fish on platter with raw onion rings and pour sauce on top.

90

MARINATED FLOUNDER WITH CUCUMBER SAUCE

Marinade:

1 lb flounder fillets

1/2 c lemon juice

1/4 t tarragon

1/4 c corn meal

1/4 c wholewheat flour

1/4 t tamari

1/2 c sesame oil

Marinate flounder in lemon juice and tarragon for 10 minutes, then drain and dip in a mixture of corn meal, flour and tamari. Saute in oil until golden brown, about 4 minutes.

Sauce:

1/2 c yogurt

1 T lemon juice

dash paprika

small cucumber, finely chopped

1 T chives

1/2 t dill

1 t kelp

Serve with Cucumber Sauce: Combine yogurt, lemon juice, cucumber, paprika, chives, dill and kelp. Serves 4.

91

SALMON SOUFFLE

2 T corn germ oil
2 T wholewheat flour
1 c milk
2 egg yolks, beaten
1/2 t sea salt
1/4 t nutmeg
2 c cooked salmon, flaked
2 egg whites, stiffly beaten

Make white sauce by stirring flour into heated oil and gradually adding milk. Slowly add small amount of sauce to egg yolk and then stir yolks into sauce. Add salt, nutmeg, pepper, salmon, and fold in egg whites.

Bake in casserole at 325° for 45 minutes.

Serve the souffle with stewed tomatoes, creamed onions, a green vegetable and fruit salad. Serves 4-6.

SCALLOPS COQUILLE

2 lb scallops
1 onion, chopped
2 c dry white wine
1/4 c sesame oil
1/4 c wholewheat flour

1-1/2 c milk
1/2 c powdered milk
1/4 c Parmesan, grated
1/2 c yogurt

Wash and remove shells of scallops. Simmer scallops, onion, and wine in saucepan for about 10 minutes or until scallops are opaque. Remove scallops and onion. Cut scallops into small pieces. Continue cooking wine until it measures 1/2 cup.

Heat oil in saucepan and stir in flour gradually, making a smooth roux. Combine milk and powdered milk, add a small amount to the roux and blend thoroughly; then add remaining milk gradually while stirring. Cook until mixture thickens. Beat in half the Parmesan cheese and the wine, then the scallops and onions. Blend the other half of the Parmesan cheese with the yogurt and spoon into warm mixture. Serve over long grain brown rice. Serves 6.

4 sole fillets
1 c milk
1/2 c wholewheat flour
1/4 c powdered milk
1/4 c sesame oil
1/2 c butter
1/4 c almonds, slivered

Place fillets in a dish and add milk to cover. Let stand for one hour then drain and dredge in flour mixed with powdered milk and seasonings. Saute in oil until golden brown, about 5 minutes on each side.

Wipe out skillet and add butter. When foamy add almonds. Pour over fish and serve with lemon wedges, boiled potatoes, green vegetables, and a fruit salad.

Serves 4.

CHICKEN CREOLE

3 lb fryer chicken, cut up
1/4 c wholewheat flour
1/2 c sesame oil
1 green pepper, chopped
1 large onion, chopped
1 stalk celery with tops, chopped

1 c tomatoes, pureed
1/4 t sea salt
2 T nutritional yeast
1/4 t oregano
1/4 t basil
1 bay leaf

Dredge chicken pieces in flour and brown in oil. Remove from pan.

Saute onions, green pepper, and celery until tender. Pour off fat. Return chicken to skillet. Add remaining ingredients. Cook over low heat, covered, for 30 minutes, then uncover and cook 30 minutes longer. Serves 4-6.

2 c rice, cooked
1/4 c olive oil
4 c stock
1 t saffron
2 c cooked chicken, in pieces
garlic clove, minced
1 c fresh green peas
2 red peppers, sliced
6 artichoke hearts
8 raw shrimp
16 clams in shells

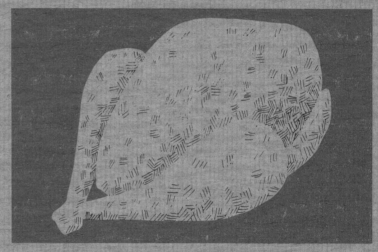

Brown rice in olive oil then add stock in which saffron has been dissolved.
Add all ingredients except shrimp and clams; cover and bake at 350° for 15 minutes. After 15 minutes, add raw shrimp and clams and continue to bake for 10 minutes more. Serves 8.

CHICKEN LIVERS WITH PILAF

Livers:
24 chicken livers, cut in half
1/4 c wholewheat flour
2 T butter

Season livers with salt then coat in flour. Brown in butter, cooking about 1-1/2 minutes on each side.

Pilaf:

1/2 c hulled barley	1/4 c onion, minced	1 t butter
1/4 c millet seed	2 T parsley, chopped	1/4 t thyme
1 c bouillon	pepper	1/4 c almonds, slivered

Serve with pilaf: Into boiling bouillon slowly add barley and millet, reheating to boiling. Lower temperature and simmer 15 minutes. Add onion, parsley, pepper, butter, and thyme; simmer 5 minutes more. Sprinkle with almonds, serve.

CHICKEN PAPRIKA

1 small onion, chopped
6 T butter
1 c wholewheat flour
2 t sea salt
6 t paprika
2-3 lb frying chicken, cut up
1-1/2 c plus 2 T bouillon
1/3 c cream
1/3 c Yano, brewed
1-1/2 c yogurt

Saute onion in 2 tablespoons butter until soft but not brown. Remove.

Combine the flour (reserving 2 tablespoons for later use), salt, and paprika in a paper bag, add chicken pieces and shake gently.

Brown poultry in 2 tablespoons butter, then add 2 tablespoons bouillon and cook covered over low heat until chicken is tender or about 40 minutes.

In a saucepan heat 2 tablespoons butter and blend in reserved flour. Add 1-1/2 cups bouillon, cream, and Yano, stirring over low heat until smooth and thickened.

Remove from heat and gradually stir in yogurt. Pour sauce over chicken. Serve over long grain brown rice with green vegetables, pickled beets, a fruit salad, and cheese wedges. Serves 4.

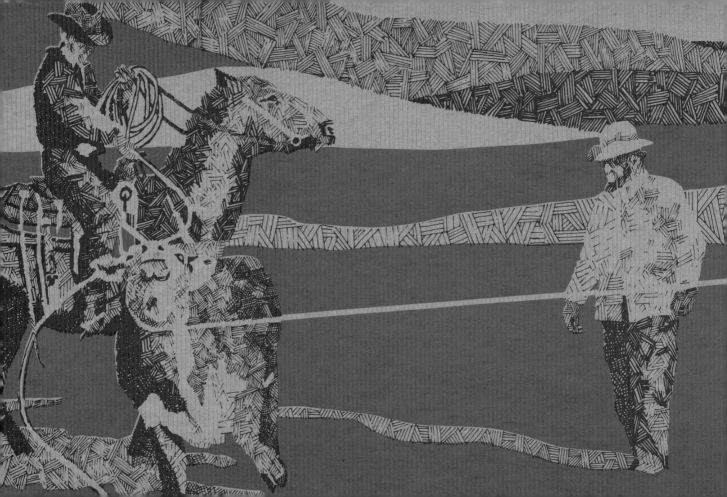

Meat Entrees

Most homemakers agree that for optimum health we ought to eat meat at least once a day. Simply cooked meats — roasts, steak, chops, hamburger — satisfy both nutritional need and taste. Any of us who has cooked for any time at all has a variety of ways of serving meats simply and interestingly.

With a commitment to natural foods as a way of better living you need invest only a little extra effort to find and cook with natural cheeses, more nutritional, organically grown vegetables, fertile eggs, and wholewheat flours, and you can do the same thing in the meat department.

For variety and pleasure, dishes like chili con carne, a lamb stew or a beef stroganoff provide exciting flavors.

Furthermore, sauced and simmered dishes like these are easy on your budget because they require less expensive cuts of meat or less per serving.

The protein value doesn't change with the cut of meat -- you get the same amount per pound when you buy an inexpensive cut as when you splurge on prime or choice cuts.

Since the less expensive grade comes from an older animal you must cook it more slowly and gently to nurture top flavor and tenderness.

Happily, by choosing these less expensive cuts you have money in your budget to buy the slightly more expensive organically-raised meats now available at natural food stores.

When you've joined the natural foods revolution you by-pass mass produced supermarket meats packaged in plastic, and instead, choose your meat from a natural food store or at least from a reliable butcher who knows something about how his meat was raised. The natural food store may be easier to find than a live, reliable butcher but either is worth the search -- and regular patronage.

Meat sold in natural food stores comes from animals raised on organic, natural feed. They have been free to graze and to choose instinctively from the land what is good for their growth.

On the other hand, the meat in most supermarkets comes from animals mass-produced by artificial insemination; animals that have been fed artificial chemical foods filled with additives; animals never free to graze. These animals have been slaughtered under tranquilizers, their meat then dipped in antibiotics to prolong shelf life.

These varied chemicals, artificial hormones and antibiotics pass from the meat into human bodies, possibly causing cancer, sterility and other not fully known, bodily defects.

The recipes which follow in this section do call for organically raised meats but you will note that many of them also suggest the inclusion of other natural foods.

JAMBALAYA

2 slices bacon
1 onion, sliced
1 bell pepper, diced
clove garlic, minced
1 t wholewheat flour
2 tomatoes, mashed

1/3 c stock
3 c cooked rice
2 c leftover veal, lamb, beef or ham
1/4 t rosemary
parsley

Render bacon and add onion, pepper and garlic, sauteing until golden.

Stir in flour; add tomato pulp and stock. Bring to a boil, then add cooked rice, meat, and rosemary. Stir over low heat for 10 minutes.

Sprinkle with parsley. Serve with corn on the cob, an avocado salad, fruit, cheese, and crackers. Serves 4-6.

LAMB STEW

2 lb shoulder of lamb, cut for stew
2 T corn germ oil
1/4 t date sugar
1 T wholewheat flour
2 c lukewarm water
1 c bouillon

1 onion
1 bay leaf
1/4 t thyme
1/2 t sea salt
12 medium potatoes,
    peeled and quartered

Heat oil and add meat, cooking until browned on all sides. Add sugar and cook 3 minutes, stirring constantly. Pour off fat and sprinkle meat with flour and cook until brown, stirring constantly. Add water, bouillon, onion, bay leaf, thyme, and salt. Bring to a boil, then cover and simmer 1 hour. Add potatoes and cook one hour more. Serves 4-6.

HUNTER'S STEW

1 c onion, chopped
2 T corn germ oil
1 small head cabbage, shredded
1 qt sauerkraut
6 large mushrooms, sliced
4 c leftover meat, diced
1 c bouillon .

2 sour apples, peeled and diced
4 prunes, pitted and soaked
2 tomatoes, pureed
bay leaf
1 t sea salt
3/4 c red wine
garlic clove, crushed

Cook onion in oil until golden brown.

Use 3-quart casserole, and add all ingredients except wine and garlic. Place covered in 300° oven and cook for 2 hours. Add wine and garlic and continue cooking for 20 minutes. Serves 8.

This stew can be prepared several days ahead and reheated to enhance flavor. Serve with wild rice or roasted potatoes and a fruit salad with cheese dressing. Serves 4-6.

MEAT LOAF

1 lb ground beef
2 T parsley, chopped
1 T corn germ oil
1/4 c soy grits, soaked in 1/2 c water
1 onion, grated
2 tomatoes, pureed
1 t lemon juice
1/2 c wheat germ
1 t tarragon

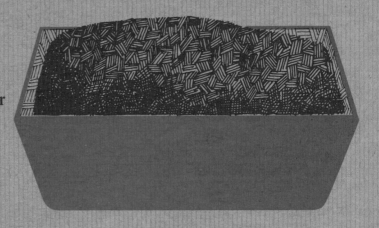

Combine all ingredients and shape into loaf. Bake in 350° oven for one hour. Baste occasionally with a tablespoon or two of bouillon. Serve with green vegetables, a baked sweet potato and Waldorf or other fruit salad. Serves 4.

CHILI CON CARNE

2 c pinto beans, cooked
1 large onion, sliced
1 green pepper, chopped
1 lb ground beef
3 T olive oil
1 c tomato sauce
1 can tomato paste
1/2 t cumin, oregano, red pepper, and bay leaf
2 T chili powder
3 T nutritional yeast

Bring one quart of water to a boil and slowly, so boiling does not stop, add beans. Reduce heat immediately after all beans are in water and simmer 2 to 2-1/2 hours.

Saute onions, green pepper, and beef in hot oil. Add tomato sauce, tomato paste, nutritional yeast, seasonings, and cooked beans. Simmer 1 hour. Serves 6.

HAM WITH CUMBERLAIN SAUCE

6 servings of ham
1 t dry mustard
1 T honey
1/4 t ginger
cayenne
1/4 t salt
1/4 t cloves
1 c red wine
1/2 c raisins
2 t arrowroot
2 T cold water
1/4 c red currant juice
1/4 c orange juice
2 T lemon juice
1 T lemon rind, grated

Sauce: Combine mustard, honey, ginger, cayenne, salt, cloves, wine, and raisins; simmer covered for 8 minutes. Dissolve arrowroot in water and stir into sauce. Let simmer for 2 minutes longer, then add currant, orange, and lemon juice plus the lemon rind.

Place slices of ham in a casserole and top with sauce. Bake 1 hour at 300°.

Serve with au gratin potatoes, zucchini or asparagus, and a cabbage slaw.

Serves 6.

BEEF STROGANOFF

1-1/2 lbs round steak
3 T wholewheat pastry flour
3 T corn germ oil
1 onion, thinly sliced
1 c mushrooms, chopped
1 c bouillon

1/2 t basil
1/2 t tamari
1/4 c sherry
1 c yogurt
1 T kelp powder

Cut round steak into 3 inch strips, 1/2 inch wide by 1/2 inch thick. Dredge in wholewheat flour and brown with onions in hot oil for 5 minutes. Add mushrooms, bouillon, basil, tamari, sherry and simmer 20 minutes more.

Stir kelp into yogurt, then add yogurt mixture to hot mixture off the fire.

Serve over wholewheat or sesame flour noodles with Oriental carrots, and a Green Goddess salad. Serves 6.

INDONESIAN BEEF STEAK

1-1/2 lbs sirloin steak
1 T tamari
1 T lemon juice
1 T honey
1 t caraway seed
1 t coriander
1 t garlic salt
1 c stock
1 T lemon juice
3 T peanut butter
1 T cayenne

Combine first six ingredients and marinate beef for one hour.

Blend the stock, lemon juice, peanut butter, and cayenne.

Broil meat to desired doneness and the moment you remove it from broiler spread with the peanut butter mixture. Serves 4.

BEEF WITH SAUERKRAUT & YOGURT

2-3 lbs lean stewing beef
1/4 c corn germ oil
2 onions, sliced
1 clove garlic, mashed
1 t sea salt
1 t paprika

2 T honey
1 c tomatoes, pureed
1 c water
2 c sauerkraut
1 c yogurt

Saute meat in oil until brown. Remove and set aside.

Add onions to skillet, cooking 5-6 minutes until golden. Return meat to skillet and add garlic, salt, paprika, honey, tomatoes, and water. Stir. Cover tightly and simmer slowly for 30 minutes.

Add sauerkraut and cook gently until meat is tender, about 2-1/2 hours. Just before serving, remove from heat and stir in yogurt.

Serve with brown rice, noodles or boiled potatoes, buttered carrots, and a molded fruit salad. Serves 4-6.

 BEEF STEW BURGUNDY

2 lbs beef chuck, cut into 1-1/2 inch cubes
2 T peanut oil
1 clove garlic
1 medium onion, sliced
2 c stock
1 c burgundy
3 T nutritional yeast
1 t thyme, oregano and vege-salt
1 lb small white onions

Brown meat in oil. Add garlic, sliced onion, vegetable stock, and wine; simmer covered for 2-1/2 hours. During the last 30 minutes of cooking, add the nutritional yeast, seasonings, small onions, and more wine if needed.

Serve with boiled potatoes, green peas, and a mixed green salad. Serves 6.

MONGOLIAN HAMBURGER

2 lbs round steak
1 t powdered ginger
4 t black pepper
1/2 t tamari
1 T & 1 t butter
1 T lemon juice
2 T burgundy
chives & alfalfa sprouts

Mix beef with ginger, shaping into four patties. Sprinkle with tamari and pepper.

In a large skillet, sprinkle a layer of salt and place over high heat. When salt begins to brown add meat and cook until well browned; turn.

When done, place a teaspoon of butter on each hamburger, add the lemon juice, and wine. Remove patties from skillet. Lower heat and swirl juices in pan. Pour over meat. Garnish with chives and alfalfa sprouts.

Salads

Dandelion, kale, chicory, endive, romaine, escarole — green leaves cherish the greatest concentration of vitamins and minerals of any fresh food.

Pick some of each, wash them quickly, then let the leaves get crispy in your refrigerator. Tear the leaves gently into a big wooden salad bowl, then coat the leaves with oil by turning and tossing each with wooden spoon and fork. Add a touch of vinegar, a smattering of tarragon or thyme, a sprig of mint or fresh rosemary, some alfalfa sprouts, seeds or raw vegetables, and serve THE PERFECT SALAD!

No salad is better than its greens and no salad beats the green salad, especially when you use a variety of leaves mingled with carefully chosen herbs, seeds, vegetables, and dressing. Choose greens and vegetables that are organically grown in soil free from chemical fertilizers — vegetables that are untouched by chemical sprays and paraffin waxes to make them look pretty.

Rinse vegetables and leaves just before use, drying them carefully to avoid any loss of water-soluble vitamins. (Never soak leaves or vegetables to make them

121

crispy). Use cold-pressed unrefined oils in your salad dressing because vegetable oils are often your only source of vitamin F — unsaturated fatty acid. Vary the oils, choosing walnut oil one day, a safflower or peanut oil the next.

For variety serve one of the popular vegetable, bean, pasta, fruit, or cheese salads. Experiment with a new dressing. Make your own mayonnaise. Probably no food you serve reveals more about you than your salads. For each tells about you in the care you take to prepare it, the imagination you use in combining ingredients, the colors and textures you choose, the subtlety or gusto of your dressings.

3 T agar-agar flakes or gelatin
3/4 c cold water
1-1/2 c boiling stock
1-1/2 c Green Goddess salad dressing*
10 oz broccoli, and/or cauliflower, chopped and cooked
1/3 c Parmesan cheese, grated

*See recipe for Green Goddess salad dressing on page 138.

Place agar-agar flakes in a blender and pour cold water on top, allowing to stand for several minutes. Add stock, blending until gelatin dissolves; use a rubber spatula to push granules down sides into mixture. When dissolved, add salad dressing and blend until smooth. Chill until slightly thickened, then stir in vegetables and cheese. Turn into six-cup mold. Chill until firm. Serves 8.

MACARONI

1-1/2 t onions, minced
2 T cider vinegar
2 t paprika
1 t tamari
1 c yogurt
2 T lemon juice
8 oz wholewheat macaroni, cooked
1/4 c green peppers, chopped
1/2 c black olives, sliced
3 hard boiled eggs, sliced

Add onion to the vinegar and let stand for a few minutes, then blend in the yogurt, tamari, lemon juice, and paprika. Pour over the macaroni. Stir in the peppers, olives, and eggs. Garnish with tomato slices. Serves 4.

2 c dried peas or garbanzos, soaked overnight
2 anchovy fillets
1 t green onions, chopped
2 T parsley, chopped
1/2 c yogurt
1 t sea salt
1 T lemon juice

Cover peas with water and bring to a boil. Drain. Add water to cover again and bring to a boil again. Turn down heat and simmer 1 to 1-1/2 hours or until tender.

Chop anchovy fillets and combine with remaining ingredients and peas. Chill for several hours. Serve on lettuce leaves, garnishing with sliced cooked beets, hard-boiled egg slices, and cubes of cheese. Serves 6.

 COLE SLAW

6 c cabbage, finely shredded	1/2 c cold water
2 t wholewheat flour	2 egg yolks, beaten
1/2 t sea salt	1/4 c cider vinegar
1/4 t paprika	1 T butter
1/2 t caraway seeds	1/4 c yogurt
2 T honey	

Combine flour, salt, paprika, caraway seeds and honey in a saucepan. Stir in cold water, beaten egg yolks, and vinegar. Cook over low heat or in a double boiler, stirring constantly until smooth and thick. Remove from heat and stir in the butter. Let cool, then blend in the yogurt.

Measure cabbage into a large salad bowl and pour on the dressing, tossing lightly. Serves 6.

Vary this basic cole slaw by adding chopped nuts, raisins, shredded carrots or apples, chopped celery, and alfalfa sprouts. Use green or red cabbage or combine the two.

GUACAMOLE

2 T agar-agar flakes or gelatin
2 c cold water
1 t tamari
2 T butter
1/4 onion, chopped
2 t curry powder

dash cayenne
1/2 c honey
2 c yogurt
2 c ripe avocados, mashed
2 T lime or lemon juice

Saute onions in butter. Add curry powder.

Combine tamari, honey, gelatin, water, and juice in a saucepan and cook until gelatin dissolves. Remove from heat. Add onions.

With a rotary beater, beat in yogurt and avocados; blend until smooth. Turn mixture into a 1-1/2 quart mold. Chill for several hours. Unmold and garnish with red peppers and cherry tomatoes. This is a good dish to serve with leftover slices of cold roast lamb, pork, turkey, or chicken. Serves 8.

4 c potatoes, cooked and diced
1 c cucumber, diced
1/4 c chives, minced
1/2 t celery seed
1-1/2 t sea salt
1/2 c cashew butter
1 c Tofu mayonnaise
1 T paprika
1/4 c cider vinegar or pickle juice
3 hard cooked eggs
pickles

Combine potatoes, cucumbers, chives, celery seed, salt, and diced egg whites. Mash yolks and mix with the cashew butter, mayonnaise, paprika, and vinegar. Pour over the potato mixture and chill. Garnish with sliced pickles.
Serves 8-10.

 LIMA BEAN

2-1/2 c lima beans, soaked overnight
lettuce leaves
parsley, chopped
alfalfa sprouts
chives, chopped

Cook beans by slowly adding them to 1 quart boiling water. Reduce heat immediately after all beans are in water and cook for 2 to 2-1/2 hours or until tender.

Combine lima beans with 1/4 cup French Dressing and serve on lettuce, garnishing with parsley, alfalfa sprouts, and chives.

Serve with French Dressing (see page 139) to which you've added a dash of curry and garlic salt. Serves 4-6.

CRANBERRY-APPLE

2 T agar-agar flakes or gelatin
2 c apple juice
1 c cranberries, sweetened with honey
2/3 c pineapple, diced
1/4 t sea salt
2/3 c grapefruit sections, diced
1 c celery, chopped
2 T honey

Soften gelatin in a half cup of apple juice. Heat remaining juice and add to gelatin. Mash cranberries and add to gelatin with other fruits, celery, and honey. Pour into 1-1/2 quart mold. Chill until firm. Unmold and serve with dab of yogurt. Serves 6-8.

 BLUE CHEESE

1 T agar-agar flakes or gelatin
1 c cold milk
1/4 t sea salt
1 c yogurt
1/2 c Blue cheese, crumbled
2 c cottage cheese
1 T onion, minced
1/2 c celery, diced
1/2 c cucumber, peeled and diced
1/2 c alfalfa sprouts
1/2 c sliced radishes

Sprinkle gelatin on milk and place over heat until dissolved. Remove from heat, add salt, yogurt, and mix well. Cool. Add cheeses, onion, celery, cucumber, sprouts, and radishes. Turn into mold; refrigerate for several hours. Serves 8.

132

2 T agar-agar flakes or gelatin
1-1/2 c boiling water
3/4 c grapefruit juice
1 T lime juice
1/4 t sea salt
1/3 c walnuts, broken
1/2 c grapes, halved
1/2 c red apples, unpeeled and diced
2 grapefruit, sectioned
1/4 c apple concentrate

Dissolve gelatin and salt in boiling water. Add grapefruit juice and lime juice. Chill until thickened. Stir in fruits, walnuts, and apple concentrate. Pour into 1-1/2 quart mold and chill several hours until firm. Unmold and frost with softened cream cheese mixed with yogurt. Serves 6-8.

 **WALDORF**

4 apples, chopped
2 stalks celery, diced
1/2 c walnuts, chopped
3/4 c yogurt
1 t lemon juice

Combine apples, celery, and lemon juice. Stir in walnuts and moisten with yogurt. Serve on lettuce leaves, garnishing with walnut halves, or Tokay grapes that have been halved and seeded. Serves 6.

COTTAGE CHEESE

1 lb cottage cheese
1 green bell pepper, chopped
1/2 c chives, chopped
1/2 c alfalfa sprouts
1/2 t caraway seeds
1/2 t sea salt
lettuce leaves

Mix cottage cheese with peppers, chives, sprouts, and sea salt. Center a mound of the mixture on lettuce leaves and garnish with hard-cooked egg slices, tomatoes, and cucumber. Top with a dab of Tofu mayonnaise. For a gourmet touch, mix 2 T of brandy with cottage cheese mixture.

GREEN GODDESS DRESSING

1 c mayonnaise
1 T anchovy paste
3 T tarragon vinegar
2 T parsley, minced
2 T green onion, minced
1/4 t sea salt
dash pepper

Combine all ingredients in blender and mix until smooth. This rich dressing is used on the Green Goddess Salad and also can be used on any vegetable or plain lettuce salad, especially with hard-cooked eggs and tomatoes.

1/2 c safflower or walnut oil
2 T vinegar
2 T lemon juice
1 t honey
1/2 t sea salt
1/2 t paprika

Combine ingredients, shake well. Makes 3/4 cup. For a variation add garlic, minced onions or chives, chopped green olives, pureed tomato, or minced peppers. Experiment with herbs by adding a 1/2 t of tarragon, dill, curry, dry mustard, basil, marjoram, oregano, or celery salt. Use seeds for added interest, a teaspoon of celery, poppy or sesame, or a tablespoon of sunflower seeds.

HONEY-ORANGE DRESSING

2/3 c French dressing
2 T honey

2 T orange juice
3/4 t paprika

Combine all ingredients and shake well. Makes 1 cup. Excellent on fruit salads.

CREAMY FRENCH DRESSING

1 t honey
1 T paprika
1 t sea salt

1/3 c vinegar
1 egg
cayenne

1 c olive or safflower oil

Combine honey and seasonings; then add vinegar and egg, beating well. Add oil 1 teaspoon at a time until 1/4 cup has been added, then gradually beat in remaining oil. Makes 1-2/3 cups.

BLUE CHEESE DRESSING

3/4 c blue cheese, crumbled
2 T vinegar
1 t anchovy paste

1 T lemon juice
1/2 c olive oil
clove garlic, minced

Mix all ingredients together, shake well. Makes 1 cup.

COTTAGE CHEESE FRENCH DRESSING

1 c French dressing
3 T cottage cheese
1 T parsley, minced
1 t dill

Combine ingredients, shake well. Makes 1-1/4 cups.

Desserts

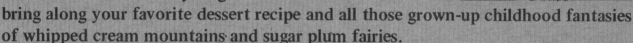

There is no need to give up any of the dulcet pleasures of desserts when you go the natural food route. Just bring along your favorite dessert recipe and all those grown-up childhood fantasies of whipped cream mountains and sugar plum fairies.

Basically, all you must do now in your new and healthier way of life is substitute honey for sugar, wholewheat pastry flour for white flour. Natural food advocates are nearly unanimous in their agreement about the harmfulness of white sugar and white flour.

With regard to white sugar they know that not only does processed white sugar contribute nothing to health, but that it is actually harmful.

Sugar in any form -- white, brown, raw -- robs the body of vitamin B, disrupts the calcium metabolism in the human body and creates upheavals in the blood sugar level.

Honey, on the other, better, hand, is a natural, unprocessed food rich in beneficial vitamins, minerals and enzymes.

For many, the fruit bowl and fruit compote make the ideal everyday dessert. But for special days and parties you simply substitute an equal or lesser amount of honey for the sugar in your dessert recipe. For each cup of honey substituted, decrease the liquid by 1/4 cup somewhere else in the recipe. Also, since baked desserts containing honey tend to brown more readily, lower the oven temperature by 25°. For crumb crusts and whipped cream concoctions when the recipe has no liquid to decrease, use date sugar.

With regard to refined white flour and even unbleached wheat flour, informed natural food advocates believe that these are both inadequate when it comes to ultimate nutrition.

First, the nutritious outer bran layer of the wholewheat kernal has been removed in milling.

Second, the vitamin-rich wheat germ has been removed to prolong shelf life.

With the richest part of the wholewheat grain discarded we no longer enjoy the tasty wholewheat kernel but instead eat a colorless, tasteless white flour.

144

To get these nutrients that nature intended us to have, always substitute wholewheat pastry flour in all recipes calling for white or unbleached wheat flour. Wholewheat pastry flour, made from a softer wheat than the wholewheat flour used for baking breads, compares nicely with white flour in texture.

With the use of wholewheat pastry flour and honey in your desserts, you're on your way. But there's more you can do to fortify your favorite desserts: substitute mineral-rich carob powder for chocolate; use a coffee substitute, such as Yano, in your gelatins, pies, and mousses; add extra powdered milk to any recipe calling for milk; use corn germ oil in place of butter; use yogurt instead of sour cream, and generally feature fruits and nuts.

CHEESE CAKE

4 eggs
1/4 c wholewheat pastry flour
1/4 t sea salt
2/3 c honey
2 T lemon juice
1/2 t lemon rind
3/4 c yogurt
2 c cottage cheese, small curd
8 oz cream cheese, softened

Beat eggs until thick, add honey, flour, salt, lemon juice, and rind. Blend cream cheese, cottage cheese, and yogurt then add to the egg mixture. Blend all. Pour into graham cracker crust. (To make crust, crumble 18 graham crackers with rolling pin and stir in 1/4 c date sugar, 1/2 cube melted butter, and 1/2 t cinnamon.) Bake at 325° for 1 hour. Serve with dab of whipped cream or with yogurt sweetened with honey. Add a few strawberries or soaked dried cherries for color.

CHOCOLATE CHIP COOKIES

1 c plus 2 T wholewheat pastry flour
1/2 t baking soda
1/2 t sea salt
1/2 c butter, softened
6 T honey
6 T date sugar
1/2 t vanilla
1/4 t water
1 egg, beaten
6-oz carob bits or chocolate

Combine butter, honey, date sugar, vanilla, and water, beating until creamy. Add the beaten egg, then the flour mixture. Stir in one 6-oz package of carob bits or chocolate bits.

Drop by teaspoonfuls onto greased cookie sheet. Bake at 350° for 10 minutes.

CHESS PIE

Shell:

1 T honey	1 egg yolk	lemon rind, grated
1/4 c oil	1 c wholewheat pastry flour	

For shell, blend honey, oil, and yolk, then stir in flour and lemon rind. Pat dough in unoiled pan. Chill.

Filling:

2 eggs, beaten	1/3 c date sugar	1/2 c seedless golden raisins
1-1/2 T wholewheat pastry flour	1/2 t sea salt	1 c pitted dates, cut up
	1 t vanilla	1 c walnuts, broken
1/3 c honey	1 c heavy cream	

Make the filling by combining the flour, honey, date sugar, and salt. Add this mixture to the eggs while beating. Stir in vanilla, cream, raisins, dates, and walnuts. Spoon into pie shell. Bake in a 350° oven for 50-60 minutes. Serves 8.

1/2 c corn germ oil
2/3 c honey
1 egg, beaten
1 c wholewheat pastry flour
1/2 t sea salt
1 t cinnamon
1 t nutmeg
2 c apples, unpeeled and chopped
1 c currants, soaked
1 c pecans, broken

Mix all ingredients and pour into 9-inch layer cake pan, greased and floured. Bake for 1 hour at 350°. Serve with whipped cream to which pulverized mint has been added.

 # DATE NUT CAKE

1/2 c dates, halved
1/2 lb walnuts, broken
2/3 c wholewheat pastry flour
2 T honey
3/4 t sea salt
3 eggs, separated
1 t vanilla
1/4 c apple juice

Mix dates, walnuts, flour, honey, and salt. Add beaten egg yolks, vanilla, and apple juice.

Beat egg whites until stiff and fold into mixture. Pour batter into a greased cake or loaf pan. Bake in a 300° oven for 45 minutes. Serve frosted with softened cream cheese.

CHESTNUT TORTE

Pastry:
1-1/2 c wholewheat pastry flour
1 t sea salt
1/2 c corn germ oil
2 T cold milk

Sift flour and salt into pie pan.

Combine oil with milk, whipping with a fork until creamy. Pour over flour mixture and mix with a fork until dampened. Press into pie pan and bake in a 425° oven for 15 minutes.

Filling:

2-1/2 c chestnuts, pureed
1/2 c butter, softened
1 T yogurt
1/2 c honey
2 eggs, beaten

1/2 t cardamom
1 t vanilla
2 egg whites
4 T date sugar
apple butter

To make the filling combine chestnuts with butter, yogurt, honey, beaten eggs, cardamom, and vanilla. Beat egg whites with sugar until stiff and fold into chestnut mixture. Pour into cooked pie shell.

Bake in a 325° oven 35 to 45 minutes. Cool and spread with apple butter.

PUMPKIN CHIFFON PIE

1 T agar-agar flakes or gelatin
1/4 c cold water
3 eggs, separated
1/2 c honey
1-1/4 c pumpkin, cooked
1/2 c milk
1/2 c milk powder
1/4 t salt
1/2 t cinnamon
1/2 t nutmeg

Prepare pastry shell (see page 152), bake and cool.

Soak gelatin in water and add slightly beaten egg yolks, then 1/4 c honey, pumpkin, milk, milk powder, salt, cinnamon, and nutmeg. Cook in double boiler over boiling water until thick, stirring constantly. Stir in soaked gelatin and cook until dissolved. Chill.

Whip egg whites until stiff but not dry.

When pumpkin mixture begins to set, stir in 1/4 c honey and fold in egg whites. Fill pie shell. Chill. Garnish with yogurt sweetened with date sugar or with whipped cream. Serves 6-8.

 **CHOCOLATE PIE**

Crust:
18 graham crackers
1/4 c honey
1/2 c butter, melted

To make the graham cracker shell, crumble crackers with rolling pin, then add honey and butter. Pat into pie pan and bake in a 250° oven for 10 minutes. Cool.

Filling:
1/2 c carob powder
1/4 c milk
2 T powdered milk
3 oz cream cheese
1/3 c date sugar
1 c heavy cream, whipped

156

1/2 t sea salt
1/2 t vanilla

    For filling combine carob with 2 T milk and powdered milk in double boiler over boiling water and cook for a few minutes. Cool slightly.

    Combine cream cheese with date sugar and blend in remaining milk. Blend two mixtures, adding salt and vanilla, then fold in whipped cream. Spoon into piecrust which has been baked and freeze until firm.

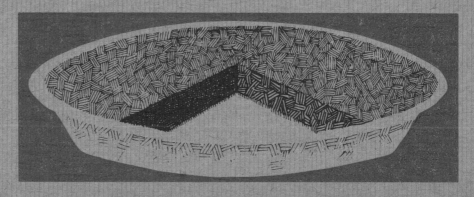

LEMON PIE IN WALNUT SHELL

Filling:

1 c honey	3 egg yolks	1 c yogurt
3 T arrowroot	lemon rind	1/4 c heavy cream, whipped
1/4 corn germ oil	3/4 c milk	
1/4 c lemon juice	1/2 c milk powder	

To make filling, mix honey and arrowroot, then add oil, lemon juice, egg yolks, rind, milk, and milk powder, cooking until thickened. Chill. Fold in yogurt and whipped cream. Spoon into baked pie shell and refrigerate for several hours.

Shell:

1-1/2 c walnuts, ground	2 T honey
1/2 c corn germ oil	

Shell: combine walnuts, oil, and honey. Press into pie plate. Bake for 8 minutes in a 400° oven.

FRUIT NUT CAKE

4 c wholewheat flour
1 c honey
1 t sea salt
1-1/2 t cinnamon
1/2 t nutmeg
1 t cloves
1/4 t mace
2 T active dry yeast
1-1/2 sticks butter
1-1/4 c very hot water
2 eggs
1-1/2 c seedless raisins
3/4 c pecans, chopped
1/4 c citron, chopped

Mix 1-3/4 cups flour with honey, salt, seasonings, and undissolved yeast. Gradually add softened butter, stirring with a wooden spoon. With an electric mixer gradually beat in the very hot water, scraping sides of bowl occasionally. Add eggs, 3/4 cup flour, or enough to make a thick batter, and beat 2 minutes at high speed. Stir in remaining ingredients.

Turn batter into greased 10-inch tube pan. Cover and let rise in a warm place until double in bulk, about 1-1/2 hours.

Bake at 350° for 45 minutes.

 **WALNUT TORTE**

Shell:
1 T honey
1/4 c oil
1 egg yolk
1 c wholewheat pastry flour
lemon rind, grated

Combine honey, oil, and egg yolk, then stir in flour and lemon rind to make shell. Add small amount of milk if necessary to make stiff dough. Pat dough in unoiled pie pan. Chill.

Filling:
1/4 c butter
3 eggs
1 c avocado honey
1/2 c date sugar

1/2 t sea salt
2 t lemon rind, grated
1-1/4 lb walnuts, chopped

Make the filling by blending the butter and date sugar. Add eggs, honey, salt, and beat until fluffy. Stir in lemon rind and walnuts. Pour into pie pan. Bake at 450° for 10 minutes then reduce heat to 350° for 30 minutes.

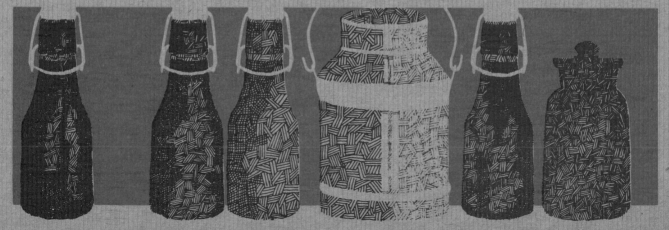

CHOCOLATE MOUSSE

1 T unflavored gelatin
1/4 c water
2 c milk
1/2 c powdered milk
3 T carob powder
1 T Yano, brewed

2/3 c honey
2 egg yolks, beaten
2 egg whites, beaten stiff
1 t vanilla
grated orange rind

Soften gelatin in water.

Heat milk with powdered milk in double boiler over boiling water and blend in carob and Yano. Bring to a boil. Stir a little of the hot mixture into the egg yolks and then combine egg yolks and hot mixture. Add honey and stir until creamy. Add gelatin. Fold in egg whites, vanilla, and orange rind. Chill for several hours.

Serve with soaked dried cherries and whipped cream. Serves 4.

 ALMOND BAVARIAN CREAM

4 t unflavored gelatin	1 t almond extract
3 T cold water	1/2 c almonds, chopped and toasted
1/4 t sea salt	2 egg whites
1-1/2 c bananas, mashed	1/2 c date sugar
1/2 c honey	3/4 c yogurt

Soften gelatin in cold water. Add salt to gelatin and place over boiling water in double boiler until dissolved. Mash bananas, add honey, date sugar, and almond extract. Combine with gelatin, place pan in a bowl of ice and stir slowly until mixture begins to thicken. Add almonds.

Chill until mixture begins to set. Fold in stiffly beaten egg whites and yogurt. Pour into cooked graham cracker crust (see page 156 for recipe).

1 c heavy cream
1 c dried apricots, apples, currants, or cherries,
    soaked and pureed
1-1/2 t lemon rind, grated
1/4 c fresh coconut, shredded

Whip cream and fold into pureed fruit. Add lemon rind. Partially freeze in freezing compartment of refrigerator for about 2 hours. Serve with a sprinkling of fresh, grated coconut and a dab of whipped cream or sweetened yogurt. Serves 4-6.

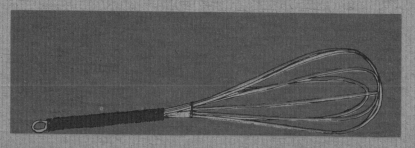

STEAMED PLUM PUDDING

1/2 c wholewheat pastry flour
1/2 lb suet, chopped
1/2 lb seeded raisins
1/2 lb currants, washed and dried
1/4 lb citron, chopped
nutmeg
1-1/2 t cinnamon
1/4 T mace
1/2 t sea salt
3 T date sugar
4 eggs, separated
2 T cream
1/4 c sherry
1-1/2 c grated rye bread crumbs

Dredge in the sifted flour and suet, raisins, currants, and citron. Resift the remaining flour with the seasonings and date sugar. Combine the dredged and sifted ingredients, then add the egg yolks, cream, sherry, and bread crumbs.

Beat the egg whites until stiff, then fold them into the raisin mixture.

Pour the batter into a greased mold or cans with tight-fitting lids, filling only about two-thirds full. Place molds or cans on a trivet in a heavy kettle over boiling water and cover kettle. Steam for 6 hours. Take the lids off the molds or cans before unmolding to allow steam to escape.

Serve with honey butter made by combining a cup of honey with a half cup of soft butter and whipped cream. Serves 12.

BROWN BETTY

2 c dessert topping (granola)
3 c apples, pared and sliced
1/3 c apple concentrate
2 T water
1/4 t cinnamon

1/2 t nutmeg
lemon rind, grated
1-1/2 t lemon juice
2 T butter

Spread a third of the Granola on the bottom of a buttered baking dish.

Saute apples in butter. Mix apples, apple concentrate, water, spices, grated rind, and juice. Put half of this mixture in the granola-lined dish, then cover with half of the remaining granola. Add the remaining fruit mixture and top with remaining granola.

Pour melted butter on top and press lightly with hands.

Cover and bake at 350° for a half hour. Serve with vanilla sauce:

VANILLA SAUCE

3 egg yolks
2 T honey
1 c cream
1/2 t vanilla
1/4 c whipped cream

Beat egg yolks with honey in top of double boiler over boiling water. Add warm cream and cook until thick, stirring constantly. Remove from heat. Add vanilla. Cool, beating occasionally. When cold, fold in whipped cream. Makes enough for six generous garnishes.

CREPES SUZETTE

Crepes:

1-1/4 c milk	2/3 c wholewheat pastry flour
1/4 c orange juice	1/2 c powdered milk
1 t orange rind	1 t sea salt
3 eggs, separated	1/4 t cinnamon

Combine milk, orange juice, and egg yolks.

Sift flour, milk powder, salt, and cinnamon. Combine the two mixtures and add orange rind.

Beat egg whites until stiff and fold into mixture. Refrigerate one hour before cooking.

Cook batter, a fourth cup at a time, in a heavy skillet brushed with oil. When crepes are lightly browned, turn and brown the other side. (If crepes stick to pan, add more milk to batter or more oil to pan.)

Sauce:
1/4 c butter
1/2 c honey
1 c orange juice
1/4 c cognac
1 T lemon rind, grated

Sauce: Combine melted butter, honey, orange juice, and cognac, then placed cooked crepes in this mixture until serving time. Simmer 5 minutes. At table add a fourth of a cup of brandy, ignite, and serve as flames die.

As an alternate, serve crepes frosted with whipped cream in which pulverized almonds have been mixed. (To pulverize almonds, put a half cup of blanched almonds in your blender and blend at top speed for 30 seconds.)

BANANA ICE CREAM

1 T unflavored gelatin
2 c light cream
1 c bananas, pureed
1/3 c honey
1/4 t sea salt
1 t vanilla

Soften gelatin in 1 cup of cream. Heat other half of cream with honey, salt, and vanilla, in a double boiler over boiling water until cream is scalded but not boiling. Remove from heat and add gelatin mixture and bananas.

Chill. When thickened, turn into blender and beat. Freeze. Serves 6.

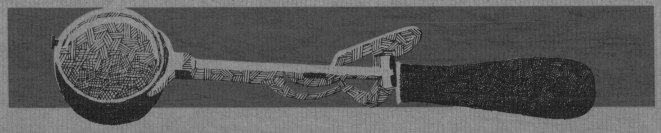

INDEX